On his high school days: *"Yeah, I was the kid who played games with all my nerd friends. You know, the kind who played Dungeons & Dragons and ate a lot of Twinkies. That was me . . ."*

On sitcoms: *"I gotta tell you the truth. I really think that a lot of them are horrid and I can't stand to watch them."*

On success: *"No, I haven't changed one bit. I'm still a common guy, a man of the people. I get my own limo door; the guy doesn't have to get out and come open it for me . . ."*

After near cancellation, his show has shot into the top 20 to become a bonafide big hit. After countless low-paying stand-up gigs, his brand of comedy is now as well known as his white shirts and skinny ties. And after years of feeling like an "outsider" under pressure to fit in, Drew Carey has stayed true to his roots—and triumphed.

This fascinating biography reveals . . .

· The true story behind his tabloid exploits

· How his comedy career—and a long car ride—strained his first serious romantic relationship

· How he focused on partying during his student years at Kent State . . . and what he thinks about those days now

· Why *The Drew Carey Show* endured unfair comparisons to *Friends* . . . and how it proved itself a unique success

· and more

HOME BREWED:
The Drew Carey Story

KATHLEEN TRACY

BOULEVARD BOOKS, NEW YORK

HOME BREWED: THE DREW CAREY STORY

A Boulevard Book / published by arrangement with
the author

PRINTING HISTORY
Boulevard edition / November 1997

The Putnam Berkley World Wide Web site address is
http://www.berkley.com

ISBN: 1-57297-361-7

BOULEVARD
Boulevard Books are published by The Berkley Publishing Group,
a member of Penguin Putnam Inc.,
200 Madison Avenue, New York, New York 10016.
BOULEVARD and its logo
are trademarks belonging to Berkley Publishing Corporation.

PRINTED IN THE UNITED STATES OF AMERICA

10 9 8 7 6 5 4 3 2 1

HOME BREWED:
The Drew Carey Story

ONE

Growing up in the Great Lakes region is a study in endurance. The summers are hot and uncomfortable, the air heavy with humidity. The mere act of trying to blow-dry your hair can turn into a marathon event and in the end, your scalp will end up singed but your hair will still be damp and fuzzy. After a week or so of beautiful autumn weather, clouds color the sky a disheartening dishwater gray and winds from the north skip over the water and turn everything in sight frigid.

One of the favorite pastimes for kids is to stand outside and show each other how their nostrils freeze shut when they sniff. This is why those who live in cities like Chicago or Cleveland pride themselves on their toughness and mettle. The conventional wisdom is, learning to cope with the elements builds character—which is probably why Southern Californians are viewed as suspect by anyone who owns a pair of mittens.

Carey readily admits that not even natives like Cleveland, notorious for bitter cold weather. For residents of the Great Lake states, threats of global warming are a cruel tease. "All I do here in the winter is stand outside with an aerosol can, spraying it into the air like this: *pssssssssss*. That's right. Fuck the grandkids, I'm cold *now*."

Welcome to the world of Drew Carey.

"I'll tell you, growing up there helped shape my world-view and my sense of humor. In my family, we didn't think much past next winter. My friends and I didn't think beyond next week. We were clueless, but we had a no-bull approach to life, and I never want to lose that," says Carey, who has gone to great lengths to keep those early life influences near and dear—more so than most people would think neces-sary.

In addition to the parents/childless grouping, the modern world is divided into two other types of people. There are the nonmigratory ones who live and die within a hundred miles of where they were born, and then there are those who get the hell out of town before the ink is dry on their diploma. Those who stay look their roots in the face on a daily basis and pass the local culture down to the next generation. Those waving good-bye look for new roots and a change in lifestyle from the one they've known. But even among those who flee is the recognition that they have been irrevocably shaped by their hometown experiences. Be-cause of that permanent umbilical bond, most harbor some sentiment for the old neighborhood. Over time and with distance, nostalgic and pleasant childhood memories float to the surface like old Polaroids we come across in a desk— nice to look at, but we wouldn't want them framed over the mantel. Few people who leave their hometowns behind to follow their individual yellow brick roads ever come back emotionally, much less try to straddle two worlds.

Then you have Drew Carey. Ambition and drive may have lured him to Hollywood, but he continues to cling fervently (actually, "neurotically" may not be too strong a description) to his Buckeye State roots. But talk to Drew for a few minutes and you quickly realize Cleveland is more than just his hometown. It's his identity. It's his anchor. It's his port in life's storm. He bleeds Cleveland brown and gets downright testy in his geographic jingoism.

"Yeah, I sort of see myself as Cleveland's ambassador to

the nation," Carey says proudly in his trademark clipped tones, head bobbing as he talks. "The thing is, you get out to Hollywood and all of a sudden, you're so far removed from where you came from you forget who you are, man. How can anyone maintain a good sense of humor and talk about things regular people can relate to if you live so vastly differently from the way they do?

"I think success can take away your points of reference, and I'm afraid of losing that. I've seen a lot of comics who are really funny when they're first starting out and struggling. Then all of a sudden when they get their big houses and TV series and movie deals, they're not so funny anymore. So no matter how big or small my career gets, I just don't want to give up my roots."

So he keeps them within arm's distance. In fact, the set of Carey's series is a one-man salute to his old stomping grounds. The sitcom is set in Cleveland, the show's bar is modeled after one of Drew's real hangouts back home and his character's house is modeled after the Carey family home he grew up in, complete with lived-in furniture.

"Yeah, sort of that Early-American-stuff-from-Sears look," Carey snorts.

Banners and paraphernalia from Cleveland sports teams adorn the walls—with the notable exception of the football Browns. After the team owner announced his intention to move the Browns to Baltimore in 1996, where they became the Ravens, Carey angrily tore down all the Browns memorabilia from the set.

"I put it in storage, along with my Browns sweatshirt," he says. "And it's too bad, because some of it was pretty nice. It really pisses me off that they left all their die-hard fans behind like that. Those are good folks they dumped. But you know what? Cleveland is just fine with or without the Browns. It's a great town, with real down-to-earth people. None of that glamour shit there.

"I hate L.A. It's such a dangerous, hateful place. But in Cleveland, if you walk to the public square, you won't find any bums or gangs. Nobody bothers anyone else, so you can go there and enjoy it as a park. In Cleveland, I don't have to dodge a bunch of homeless guys when you go to a restaurant to get something to eat the way I do in L.A. Even though Cleveland is a big city, it's got a small, hometown feel. That's why I love it so much.

"Cleveland is the best of everything."

Another Cleveland native suggests Carey may be seeing through rose-colored pop-bottle glasses.

"Cleveland's not Shangri-la. It's got its fair share of crime, and the people there have their own brand of classism. For example, if you come from a less acceptable area of town, you're forever branded as being from the wrong side of the tracks. No matter how well you do for yourself in life, other people from Cleveland still sort of label you by where you lived. So while Cleveland may not have movie studios and Beverly Hills and stars living there, it still has a lot of pretensions and neighborhood hierarchies of its own."

But Drew dismisses any criticism of his city as uninformed.

"You know what's great about this city? People here like to see a hometown guy make good. And in Cleveland, if they like you, you know it. And," he adds, "if people don't like Cleveland, they can kiss my ass."

Carey's aggressive sentimentality toward the place known as the Polka City prompted him to make a deal with his mom to buy the old family home after she remarried in 1984 and moved to a nearby town with her new husband. The thought of the place where he grew up being taken away unnerved Drew, even though he was already in his mid-twenties. And it wasn't as if the house was an architectural prize. It's a classic wooden A-frame, straight out of Main Street, USA—small, drafty and chronically cold in the wintertime.

"Oh, yeah, the house always had problems—the windows were painted shut, some of the doors wouldn't close, there were light switches that never worked—but man, there was no way I wanted that house to belong to someone else," Carey says. "That's the house I was born in and where I grew up. I have a lot of fond memories of that house and couldn't see selling it. And my mom didn't want to, either.

"I was twenty-five when my mom remarried but I was still living at home 'cause I still had no idea what I wanted to do with my life. But at least I had my room in the basement, and I didn't want to have to move. So my mom and I worked out a lease-option deal where I rented the house from her for two hundred and fifty dollars a month and that money went toward the purchase price. Houses back there don't cost anywhere near what they do in L.A. People can actually afford to buy a house in Cleveland.

"Once I started making some money doing stand-up, it was pretty easy to buy it. Then I paid off the loan with the money they paid me to do the pilot for the show."

It's ironic that Carey is so possessive of his childhood haunts, because by his own admission, he spent much of his youth being miserable. Drew was the third son of Lewis and Beulah Carey in the Old Brooklyn neighborhood of Cleveland, a solidly blue-collar enclave populated by second- and third-generation Poles, Italians and Irish Americans. Then, as now, the houses on Carey's street reflected the middle-to-lower class economics of their inhabitants. There was nothing remotely glitzy or glamorous about life there. In this world, people worked hard without complaint at the factory jobs then in plentiful supply, which enabled them to both provide for their families and have a little left over to stash away in a savings account. Vacations were luxuries few splurged on. Children were well cared for and education was stressed.

Summers were spent riding bikes or playing games with the other neighborhood kids. Even though Cleveland is on Lake Erie, few frolic in the water unless a wet suit is handy; the water is not only cold but pollution, even in the sixties, was a problem. Public pools were a much safer way to beat the summer heat. At dusk, lightning bugs would hover over the grass, and a favorite sport among children was to catch the poor creatures, scoop out their lights and wear the trophies as jewelry. After the sun set, people would relax on their front porches until dive-bombing mosquitoes forced them to go inside or to coat themselves with a can of bug repellent.

The first eight years of Drew's life were unremarkable, as far as childhoods go. He went to school and endured the teasing of his two older brothers, Neal and Roger. Self-conscious and awkward, Drew wasn't the most popular kid, but he had a circle of friends he hung out with. Even as a kid, however, Drew enjoyed solitude.

Drew's dad, Lewis Carey, was a hardworking draftsman for General Motors, meaning he made mechanical drawings for the car company. Lewis was a good-natured soul who used to entertain his children with impromptu bursts of tap dancing. Carey's most vivid memories of his dad are of him laughing and hoofing in their small kitchen. But just at the age when Drew and his father could begin to do more things together, Lewis was diagnosed with brain cancer. Laughter was suddenly in short supply in the Carey house. There was nothing doctors could do except send Lewis home to die. An eight-year-old Drew watched helplessly as his father wasted away, the cancer not only robbing him of life but of personality as well. After a slow and agonizing illness, Lewis Carey died. He was only forty-five. It was the pivotal event in Drew's childhood, and would prove to be a major influence in molding his adult personality as well. Although Carey doesn't usually talk about his feelings in public, he acknowledged the enormity of his father's death when he said, "It was the single most devastating thing that ever happened to me."

Any kid grieves over the loss of a parent, and experiences temporary but normal depression and anger. But Drew didn't snap out of it. Instead, the little boy caved in on himself. Pictures of Drew from that time show an outwardly calm but distant child. He might have been a lot better off had he been able to scream and cry his upset and shout his rage. Instead, he kept the emotional fallout internal, and in so doing took the first step on the way to the crippling adult depression that would shadow him later.

It's not that Drew didn't realize he was in trouble. Even at eight years old, he was aware enough to sense that his emotions were slipping away from his control, and it scared him: "I was miserable. I found myself getting angry and resentful of other kids just because their parents were both still alive."

Finally, the youngster told his mother he thought he should see a psychiatrist. But in 1960s Ohio, kids didn't go see psychiatrists. In general, blue-collar second- and third-generation Americans were wary of psychiatry, and many saw it as a sign of weakness or a character flaw.

Beulah Carey placated her youngest son and told him she'd look into it.

"But she never found the time to take me," Carey says.

Nor were his brothers able to offer much solace. Drew was six years younger than Roger and twelve years younger than Neal. It's hard to have a close, buddy-type relationship with such an age gap. So while his older brothers were off being teenagers, Drew was left to cope the best way he could on his own, which was to bottle up his feelings and try to ignore them.

Forced to raise her children as a widowed single parent, Beulah found work as a keypunch operator, which meant that Drew was often alone after school, a latchkey kid before the term was even invented. He'd walk to a nearby record store and buy the latest eight-track tape to listen to. Or he would go to the library after school and hide out among the books. But mostly, comedy became his imaginary best friend. He kept himself entertained by watching cartoons on television, memorizing joke books and listening to comedy albums, learning to mimic the timing and delivery. He says now that part of the reason he was so obsessed with things funny is that he thought himself to be unfunny—even though he was the class clown.

"I was always the joker, the one cracking jokes. I thought I was funny, but I always thought my friends were funnier, so I tried to make myself funnier by listening to different comedians and knowing lots of jokes. I'd listen to the morning radio shows and mimic the jokes for my friends. I thought it would make people like me more. I was kind of popular, but not really, if you know what I mean."

Being liked more by others, he figured, would help Drew like Drew more. But it didn't happen that way. Instead, Carey entered his teen years not entirely liking himself a whole lot, a typical state for most adolescents, and still deeply wounded by the death of his dad. Now in the occasionally thick-skinned world of comics, this—being an awkward teenager, not losing a parent to cancer—could be great fodder for a stand-up routine. But don't expect "Carey: The Early Years" as an HBO special anytime soon. While he has talked in interviews about being morose after losing his father, he has never delved into his psyche to share it with the world at large in his act, as Woody Allen does in his films or Rick Reynolds does in his stand-up. (Reynolds actually goes a step further and uses each stand-up routine as a mini–therapy session, sharing stories about how his marriage fell apart and therapy saved it and how he wishes he were still in love with his wife the way he was when they were first married. While it may not sound like traditional knee-slapper stuff, Reynolds presents it in a way that's hilarious. He's baring his soul about painful things everyone can relate to, but it comes out funny.)

Drew's comedy also relates to the common man, but not in an introspective way. He's more concerned with the day-to-day stuff and is out to poke gaping holes through anything or anyone that makes those not blessed with beauty or social skills or wealth feel small or less worthy. Carey channels his barbs through his sitcom character.

On women:

"The beautiful thing about sitting in this bar in Cleveland is that none of these women has a chance in hell of meeting Brad Pitt. So here's to us, their little cold splash of reality."

And money:

"Hey, I'm not looking to buy a Ferrari, but I'd like to get a few paychecks ahead. I'd like to be able to actually give a little money to charity instead of just lying about it on my taxes."

Or careers:

"When I took a job as a salesclerk, I never thought it would lead to a career, but now I'm assistant director of personnel. I have a position of indirect respect and oblique power."

A fellow comic who's worked with Carey says Drew's comedy is notable for how assiduously he avoids mentioning his family during his stand-up.

"That's something he avoids. His life is definitely not his act. In fact, his act is an avoidance of his life. His act deals with everybody else's life, not his own. Much of his act is about ridiculing those who are self-righteous and interfering, like antismokers. In his act, he'll ask for a show of hands of the smokers in the club."

Carey points out that they must know they're risking their health by smoking—because it's a fact nonsmokers never miss an opportunity to point out, as if it was late-breaking medical news.

"You're killing yourself!"

"Oh, fuck, really? Hey, honey! I almost killed myself—this guy saved my life!"

Particularly irritating to Carey is that people act so self-righteous in pointing out obvious faults, flaws, and vices, such as smoking or overeating. And to them he has these words of appreciation:

"Safety Nazis. Fuck off."

About the only thing that seems to be off-limits are family related jokes and observations. Whether it's out of deference to his family or for less warm and cozy reasons is up for debate. Once, during an on-line cyber-interview session, someone asked Carey if he was going to let any family members appear on his show.

"Are you kidding?" he responded. "I keep my family locked up—where they belong."

When another fan persisted and asked if he came from a big, loving family, Drew shot back:

"No! Now leave me alone."

Despite his adding the cyber symbol for kidding—:)—it was a telling answer.

After Lewis Carey died, life got a lot harder. Money was tight and the house suddenly seemed too small for all the baggage everyone was carrying.

"Our house was just supposed to be a 'starter house' for my parents," Carey explains. "But after my dad died we were never able to get out of there."

Drew and Roger shared a bedroom off the kitchen while Neal, pulling rank as the oldest, got the room over the porch to himself. Their mom retreated to the attic, which had been converted to another bedroom. The house didn't have a dining room so the kitchen served as the family room, where they'd eat dinner together. The most trying aspect of the house, though, was that it only had one bathroom.

"Any roadside motel has a bigger bathroom than the one we had," Carey says. "It was insane trying to get in and out of there to get ready, but we did it."

Despite the emotional hole and financial difficulties presented by Lewis's death, Beulah and her boys carried on. But a former girlfriend and still close friend of Drew's, Jackie Tough, says the impact of Lewis's death lingered and can still be seen today in some of Carey's attitudes.

"Drew's family never recovered from the loss," she says. "To this day, Drew hates holidays because they remind him of happy times with his family when his dad was alive. He doesn't celebrate them at all, because the memories are still too painful."

Recently, a fan asked Drew how he was going to celebrate the upcoming holidays, and his answer was surprisingly bitter:

"I don't celebrate Christmas," he said. "I never get presents or give them. And if I believed in Santa, I would ask that he disappear and never come back again."

TWO

In junior high, Drew presented a far different picture than he does now. *Style* magazine ("There's one magazine I shouldn't be in," Carey has quipped) printed family snapshots, and most striking is his size; in a photo from his sixteenth birthday, Drew is shown as a skinny teen, weighing in at only 123 pounds. He had long blond hair, wore glasses and had a fondness for flared pants, preferably red plaid. If there was any doubt of his probable nerd status, the pants would be Exhibit One for the charge of being fashion-challenged.

Whether his clothing style was an subconscious protest against the cool kids or, as is more likely, simply reflected his personal taste, Carey came across as a bit of an eccentric and projected the attitude that he didn't really care all that much what others thought about him.

One of Drew's big obsessions was board games. He says he was as addicted to them as kids today are to video games. In fact, he says that's probably how most of his high school classmates remember him.

"Yeah, I was the kid who played games with all my nerd friends," he says wryly. "You know, the kind who played Dungeons & Dragons and ate a lot of Twinkies. That was me.

"Battleship was another one of my favorites. Do you know that now they have Battleship for your computer? So you can spend five thousand dollars on a computer to play a ten-dollar board game. The same with solitaire—a pack of cards is only a buck-fifty."

When asked to describe his childhood in five words or less, Carey ticked off on his fingers. "Weirdo. Weirdo. Underachiever. Weirdo. Weirdo."

Despite suspecting that everyone considered him a nerd, Carey enjoyed high school well enough and he participated in extracurricular activities that showed his range of interests—he played trumpet in the school's band, and the gangly teen was also a member of the wrestling team. But one sport does not a popular jock make. Carey was still one of those kids you go to school with but never really pay attention to; they seem nice enough, but it would never occur to you to invite them to a party at your house. Years later, as you were leafing through a yearbook, he'd be the one you would look at and try to recall, and certainly wouldn't remember his name. If personality is cemented in early childhood, then high school forever shapes some core element in how we see ourselves.

"Drew was the kind of guy I'd say hello to, I'd laugh when he said something funny, but would have never in a million years hung out with him," says one acquaintance bluntly.

Happy enough with his board game chums, Drew felt sufficiently confident to try out for the school play, and to his surprise he was cast in the lead role of Rhodes High School's production of *Pirates of Penzance*.

"Even though he wasn't all that outgoing, Drew was a born ham," says a friend. "He thinks nothing about getting in front of people singing or dancing. Even as a gawky teenager, he just went for it, and he just ate up the applause he got at the end of the show. It was his first taste of having an audience in his hand, and he liked it a lot."

But is wasn't an epiphany. The smell of the greasepaint and the roar of the crowd didn't hit Carey like a bolt of lightning and steer him to his performing career. It was just a fun thing to have done. Although most actors will tell you they knew from childhood or adolescence that they had to act or that being in the high school play turned their life around, it's curious that many comics sort of fall into stand-up, rather than its being something they grew up dreaming about.

Ellen DeGeneres was drifting through a series of jobs in New Orleans when a coworker suggested she should try her hand at stand-up. Some friends were putting together a local benefit and asked her to do something onstage, and she agreed. She was so unsure of herself that she only prepared one bit, but it was enough to bring down the house—and to give birth to a career.

Brett Butler was a single mother in Texas, working as a waitress, when some of her diner customers encouraged her to sign up for a local comedy amateur night. She wrote some material, won the contest and four thousand performances later, landed her own sitcom.

Likewise, Drew didn't burn with an innate desire to get up in front of a bunch of strangers and make them laugh. He had enjoyed doing the play but never considered it remotely possible to make a career in show business, enjoyed playing the trumpet but did not have the desire, or the talent, to be a musician, and professional wrestling wasn't an option. If he could have only figured out a way to make a living playing board games, his future would have been set. But as he neared the end of high school, that future was instead a gigantic question mark.

Although he wasn't a stellar, dedicated student, Drew was bright enough that he was able to skip his senior year of high school and prepare to enter college a year earlier than most of his classmates. First, he had to decide where to go. Not wanting to stray too far from home and unable to afford a private college, he applied to Kent State University, located in Ashtabula, Ohio. Although he had absolutely no idea what he wanted to do with his life, he did know that he didn't want to end up being just a working stiff at a plant. He wanted something different; he just couldn't figure out what.

•   •   •

When Carey got to Kent State, he was a seventeen-year-old virgin who had never drank or done drugs or even used a swearword in his life—but all that was about to change.

"Yeah, I joined a fraternity when I got to college, and they couldn't believe me," Carey recalls. "They were like, *Whoa, you've never had sex? You've never got drunk?* And I was like, *No, no, no—not me.*

"Then by the end of that first year, I'd done everything. Man, I was on a quest."

Drew paints a picture of his typical Friday at college, circa 1975:

After taking a nice, long afternoon nap, he cleans up and gets ready for a night on the town, which will basically entail drinking lots of beer and going disco dancing. In his closet he's got a selection of the suffocating polyester clothes made so popular by John Travolta in *Saturday Night Fever.*

"You betcha." Carey laughs. "I had the gold chains, the bell-bottoms, everything. I was smoking, man. I had dance partners and we would practice our moves in front of the mirror and then go out to clubs and show off."

But before leaving, Carey would carefully soak himself in eye-watering amounts of Brut. He'd even massage it through his flowing blond locks.

"Some girl who liked me once told me she liked Brut, so I thought Brut was it. I had never worn cologne before and they didn't have a lot of colognes to pick from, either, back then like they do now. So I bought every Brut product they had: shampoo, soap-on-a-rope . . . hell, I probably even bought Brut underwear. My motto was, all chicks must love Brut. I thought I'd cracked the secret code to getting women.

"Man, I must have fucking reeked."

College opened up a whole new world for Drew. Away from the eyes of his mother and freed from his conservative neighborhood's unspoken-but-expected codes of behavior, Carey let loose. He discovered he loved beer, wasted no time finding a girl willing to go to bed with him and found a new group of friends who were just as interested in partying as he was. Even so, he wasn't exactly Big Man on Campus material just yet.

"I still loved my board games and had brought my favorite ones to college with me," he says. "During rush week there are all these keg parties, when you visit all the different fraternities. You go to get drunk and see which one you want to join and whether they in turn want you.

"At the rush parties, everyone sort of bullshits with each other and asks you things, like what your hobbies are. So one night I'm at the Delta Tau Delta rush party and I tell the guy about my board games and how I'm really into them."

Carey mistook the guy's polite conversation for genuine interest.

"The Delts liked me and I got invited back to the next party. Everyone else there has brought beer and is drinking, and here I come with a bunch of my games with me, like Monopoly and Risk. At first, they all kind of just stared at me. You know they were thinking, *What a nerd.* But then they said, *Oh, what the hell—let's just play.*"

The tone for his college experience was set. Partying and playing became Drew's primary activities, with academics a foggy, far-off third.

"I had a *great* time partying," Carey admits. "I had grants and loans to pay for tuition and books so I spent all my money on pitchers of beer and pizza. Man, they had the cheapest pizza at a place called the Loft. I was just seventeen, though—I really should have been in high school, but instead I was on my own at college, partying all the time."

Back home, Beulah would never have imagined the *Animal House* party hound Drew had become. While he had never been an academic all-American, she had no idea he would become so irresponsible once out on his own; he had been such a straight arrow at home. She would have been shocked to witness her son's personality about-face. It was bad enough to learn about it from afar.

Carey's college buddies weren't seeing the whole Drew picture either, though. They had no idea that underneath the jokes and partying, there was a lot of brooding anger and frustration. To his pals he was a brew-chugging, pizza-loving, happy-go-lucky kind of guy, and Drew did his best to live up to that image. But the signs were clear that something was amiss. He underwent a personality overhaul in the first few months of college. He drank too much. He showed no interest in his studies. Most telling, he was prone to abrupt anger over seemingly trivial things.

He partied at every opportunity, not only to assure himself he was having fun but because constructive soul-searching is easy to avoid after a few pitchers of beer. Looking back now, Drew says he felt emotionally adrift during those years. The future yawned in front of him and he had no idea how to fill the space. For a while, he thought he might want a career in criminal justice; he signed up for an introductory course but lost interest after the first few classes. He registered for, then dropped, a series of classes, never able to find something to hold his attention. He switched majors on a regular basis, and with each change felt more worthless. He knew he was squandering his time at college. He knew he was wasting an opportunity. It made him feel empty and edgy, but he felt helpless to change it.

"I felt I was just taking up space," Carey says.

Drew had never made a big deal about his dad's dying. He didn't dwell on it the way a more introspective person might have; he left his emotions about his father's death alone to simmer. In retrospect, it's easy for Drew to see that he was so angry at others because he had never been able to constructively channel the anger he felt at being left behind—mostly because he'd never figured out what exactly was going on. He knew he'd get angry for no reason, but didn't understand why. Like the cowboy says, you can't tame the bronco until you let it out of its stall. Most kids don't realize that it's not only normal to be mad at a parent who dies, but that it's healthy. Emotion released is emotion controlled. But since Drew couldn't express his fury against his dad, he took aim first at others, then at himself. He was eighteen the first time he tried to kill himself.

The evening started out no differently from most of his

nights at college. There was no flash-point confrontation with anyone that sent him over the edge. It was the normalcy of the scene that set Drew off.

"One night I was at this fraternity party with all these other people," Drew recounts calmly, almost like a third-person observer. "Everybody was having such a good time, I couldn't stand it. I got so mad, I could barely control my rage."

Furious, Carey went to his room and gulped down a handful of pills.

"But as soon as I took the pills, I started having thoughts like, *Is there a heaven and a hell? What's going to happen to me?* I realized I didn't want to find out. I suddenly got scared, because I thought I was going to hell. I called my fraternity brothers and they took me to a nearby health clinic, where they gave me ipecac to help me throw up."

Carey shrugged off the suicide incident. He apparently decided against seeking out psychiatric help through the school and went right back to his party animal existence. If his brush with death gave him any pause for thought, he didn't share it with anyone.

Despite admitting that concern about what happens to us after we die propelled him to call for help, Carey doesn't claim to be religious. Nor does he use his suicide attempt as the basis for any stand-up monologues, the way Richard Pryor did after he nearly incinerated himself. Carey is more circumspect. The closest he comes to dealing with the issue of death and the hereafter in a routine is when he calls the Pope on the carpet for being security-conscious, driving in the bullet-proof popemobile, surrounded by gun-toting security guards.

"Is he afraid someone is going to shoot him and that he's gonna die and go to heaven? That'd be horrible, huh?

"If the *Pope* is afraid to die, what the fuck chance do we have?"

Carey also muses over people who try and plan their demise too carefully, such as those who draw up living wills that try to anticipate any possible medical complication. Drew prefers not to dwell on the inevitable, figuring there's not much you can do about it, anyway. If it is time to go, you're gone. But he's not an advocate of rushing the process along, either.

Drew jokes that he, for one, has no intention of leaving instructions for his loved ones or doctors to pull the plug, even if he's comatose for decades.

"I'm going to enjoy my coma . . . it would be like having a government job."

Drew avoided going to class or doing any course work, and eventually the lack of study time caught up to him. Unlike high school, where even average students can coast, college is not forgiving. Drew was academically dismissed not once but twice during his time at Kent State.

"I partied so much, my grade-point average went down to .5," he says. "Even in high school, I never studied. I did my homework right before class and never paid attention, because it wasn't that hard. I had plenty of friends in college trying to help me, but I had no goals. I didn't start having goals until I was in my twenties."

After five years, Carey left Kent State without a degree. He'd never even declared a major. Now, almost twenty years later, Carey is still ambivalent about his time in college.

"I know what I should have done to graduate, and my advice to some guy sitting around drinking beer all night instead of studying would be: Either shit or get off the pot," Carey says. "Study, learn, find a major. Be there to be there or get out; you're better off saving your money.

"But," he adds, "if I could do it all over again, I wouldn't change anything. I read more and know more now. I work so hard. Society is so credential-oriented. That's why people bullshit so much on their résumés. I've always felt I have to prove I'm not stupid, since I never got my degree. But you have to let the past go and be whatever you want to be."

The trick, of course, is *knowing* what you want to be. Until he could figure it out, Drew went home and occupied his time by passing the time. One of his diversions was sports. An avid fan, he found that his beloved Cleveland teams suffered the same kind of malaise of spirit that plagued him. Instead of offering a break from daily troubles, the Cleveland Indians baseball team only added to his melancholy. Now, he jokes about the frustration of being a die-hard fan of a bad team.

"Summertime was the worst, because everybody makes fun of the Indians because, well . . . they suck. (I know they tried hard and everything, but it doesn't matter because they suck.)

Then come every September, it seemed the Indians would be near the bottom of the standings, just playing the season out, any hope for the playoffs long gone. Drew says their resignation was easy to spot.

"There's a fly ball to right field and the guy's trying to put his cigarette out before the ball gets there. Man, I'm telling you, it's so tough being a sports fan in Cleveland."

But at least the Indians' miserable seasons had a designated end and they got the chance to start all over with fresh hope every April. Drew, on the other hand, had blown off his college education and came home to no prospects and a nagging sense of failure. So he decided to try for his own fresh start and took to the road, heading west to Las Vegas.

THREE

Las Vegas has become the number one family vacation destination. Hotels took a cue from Disney and created megatheme resorts where there's something for everyone in the family. Up and down the brilliantly lit Las Vegas strip are fantasy resorts intended to transport you into another world. At the MGM Grand, kids can spend the day at the hotel's amusement park while mom and dad gamble their money away. Across the street at Excalibur, knights in armor hold jousting contests. Farther down the street a giant Egyptian pyramid rises out of the desert, shining a beacon of light into the sky so bright our astronauts can see it during their orbit. Down the strip at the Mirage, a volcano erupts every twenty minutes after dusk; during the day, guests lounge around its lake-sized pool, which has a waterfall and two giant slides. Adjacent to the pool is another pool that is home to a pair of dolphins. Next door at Treasure Island, pirates roam the grounds and several times a day a mighty ship battle is waged in a lagoon in front of the hotel between pirates and members of Her Majesty's Royal Navy. The streets are clean and well lit. Las Vegas Boulevard, which runs the length of the strip, has been carefully landscaped with leafy palm trees that were imported at great expense into the city.

But in 1980, Las Vegas was not Disneyland in the desert. The city that Bugsy Siegel built was still primarily a gambling mecca that was not very family-friendly. Although the hotels still boasted individual themes, such as the Tropicana's jungle motif and Circus, Circus' "Big Top," their reason to be was gambling, not resort park luxury. People who vacationed in Vegas were there either to see headliner shows or to gamble or to partake of the freely available sexual favors the city offered.

As a result, a much bleaker side of life was more visible on the streets of Las Vegas then. Away from the main hotels and their colorful neon decorations, most of the sidewalks were still unpaved dirt and the pretty, well-lit center median on Las Vegas Boulevard didn't exist. On these darkened walkways, vendors hawked any one of the numerous XXX-rated clubs with "live nude girls" and aggressive hookers brazenly confronted pedestrians in an attempt to drum up business. Las Vegas in 1980 had a low-life, seedy quality to it that complemented its nickname—Sin City.

Las Vegas also attracted another type: those looking to find work. A lot of money flowed through Las Vegas and there were good-paying jobs to be had. Unfortunately, there were also a lot of temptations. It was a familiar sight to see people cash their paychecks and blow all their earnings in a night at a craps or blackjack table.

The haves and have-nots are sharply defined in Las Vegas, which is perhaps why the city has a significant crime rate for a city its size. Among the locals who don't work at the casinos, there has always been a certain resentment against the high rollers who breeze into town and think nothing of dropping a couple of grand in an hour. For someone on the outside looking in, Vegas can be a demoralizing example of excess and inequity.

But for someone just pulling into town, Las Vegas at first blush is an exciting, twenty-four-hour city where the sky's the limit. Compared with Ohio, Vegas is like Oz—

somewhere over the rainbow, not of this world. It's easy to see why Drew was attracted to it—its round-the-clock activity makes it one of the premier party towns. You can always find a drink, and you never have to worry about drinking alone.

Twelve-step programs make a big deal about geography— namely, that moving won't solve your problems; they'll simply follow you wherever you go, like a troublesome shadow. For Drew, the thrill of going to the festive casinos and playing the gaming tables lasted a little while, but it wasn't long before those old feelings began to tap him on the shoulder and he found himself even more depressed than before. He found work as a bank teller and as a waiter at a Denny's, but lived like a migrant, renting a room at a cheap, dreary motel. Being around happy, jovial vacationers that were Las Vegas's lifeline only served to make Drew more morose. On the outside, though, he was still the life of the party. He made friends and they enjoyed his company. Nobody had any idea Drew was despondent enough to want to kill himself.

In an interview, former girlfriend Jackie Tough described what led up to his second suicide attempt.

"Drew was living at this fleabag motel because he didn't have enough money to rent a nicer apartment. Then one day he went out gambling and lost so much money that he couldn't even afford to pay for his hotel, so he was forced to live out of his car."

Carey commuted between his teller and waiter jobs, trying to get together enough money to rent another room somewhere.

"In his car were literally all his earthly belongings," said Tough. "One night when he was working at the restaurant, someone stole his car right out of the parking lot. All he had left was the shirt on his back and the tip money in his pocket. At that point he felt he had absolutely nothing. He just lost it."

Carey says the theft of his car was just the capper of a potpourri of issues weighing on him.

"There were all these things that seemed to say I just wasn't a good enough person," Carey recalls. "I was in great

health. I had great friends, but I hated myself so much. I had
a really bad self-image. I was ugly. I just didn't like myself
and nothing I did was good enough. I remember thinking,
*All my friends have jobs now. They're succeeding, but what
am I doing?*

"I had been getting just more and more depressed until
finally, I didn't see anything at the end of the tunnel: no
light, no food, no love—nothing."

So he popped a bottle of sleeping pills, but then, as at
college, he had immediate second thoughts.

"After I swallowed the pills, I chickened out and called
for help."

While gulping a bunch of pills once might be considered
an aberration, twice is a definite red flag. It was time for
Drew, his family and friends to stop and take stock. The big
question for those around Drew was, Why? What was so
bad and so unchangeable that Drew even entertained the
idea of dying, not once but twice?

According to mental health workers, people usually
attempt suicide to get away from some overwhelming
emotional pain.

"A person attempting suicide is often so distressed that
they are unable to see that they have other options," says
one suicide expert. "The majority of individuals who try to
take their lives do not have a diagnosable mental illness;
they are just people who at a particular time are feeling
isolated, desperately unhappy and alone. People can usually
deal with isolated stressful or traumatic events and experiences reasonably well, but when there is an accumulation of
such events over an extended period, normal coping strat-
egies can be pushed to the limit.

"And, yes, it's often the much talked about *cry for help*."

Which certainly seems to be the case with Carey. As
Graham points out, if someone really wants to kill himself
and meticulously plans it, he will more often than not
succeed. Drew's actions were impulsive and spontaneous.

"Both times Drew attempted suicide, he called his friends
to save him," Tough points out. "I think he desperately
needed to know that people cared about him. I'm convinced

his career is now going so well because of his insatiable need for attention and affection. Even so, though, Drew has been and probably always will be a sort of depressed personality."

Drew's second aborted suicide bid wasn't shrugged off. This time, Carey knew he needed help, and his family rallied around him. His brother Roger paid for Drew's bus fare back to Cleveland, and once back home Carey immersed himself in books like Dr. Wayne Dyer's *Your Erroneous Zones* and Og Mandino's *University of Success,* looking for help in locating his lost self-esteem.

Mandino is one of the most popular motivational speakers on how to achieve success, and Dyer made his fame and fortune espousing his method of managing stress and building self-worth. The "erroneous zones" of Dyer's title refers to unhealthy behavior patterns such as guilt, anger, anxiety and insecurity. Individuals are encouraged to look at their lives in positive ways, to understand that they have the power and the control to change themselves and their world if they so desire, all explained via easy-to-digest aphorisms:

> When you think positive, happy, loving thoughts, there's a different chemistry that goes into your body than when you think depressing, negative, anguished thoughts. The way you decide to think has a dramatic effect on your chemistry and on your physiology. . . .

> Advance confidently in the direction of your own dreams to live the life that you have imagined. That's when you have success. . . .

> Stop blaming your spouse for your unhappiness, your parents for your social status, the bakery for your excess weight, your childhood for your phobias, and anything else to which you assign blame points. You are the sum total of the choices you have made in your life. . . .

> We can be whatever we want to be by taking control of

our lives and learning to abandon negative thoughts and behavior patterns.

—Dr. Wayne Dyer
from an advertisement for
Your Erroneous Zones

Self-help books are often the butt of jokes, but their enduring popularity says something about the number of people in our modern culture looking for affirmation and guidance. After studying the lessons offered by Dyer and Mandino, it was clear to Carey that his very survival depended on his learning to like himself a lot better. He needed to find something that made him feel like he was a contributing member of the world and not just taking up space. When he found it, it was quite by accident.

Drew's brother Neal had moved to California several years earlier when Carey was a sophomore in college. In 1980, once he'd recovered from his Las Vegas nightmare, Drew felt well enough to take a trip to California and spend time with his brother.

Neal lived near San Diego, a smaller, cleaner, more homey version of L.A., its neighbor to the north. San Diego's port is a major, highly visible part of the city's identity, with restaurants, hotels and quaint shopping villages lining the waterfront. It's also got a lot of military offices; San Diego is a main training center for the elite Navy SEALS, and warships are commonly seen pulling in and out of San Diego Bay.

While wandering around San Diego one afternoon, Carey was inexplicably drawn into a Marine Corps Reserve recruiting office. He read the brochure and, after years of aimlessness, was attracted by the idea of enforced discipline and the challenge of cutting it as a Marine Reservist.

"The Marine Corps Reserve is critical to the Marine Corps," the brochure stated. "Without a Reserve, we could not maintain a degree of readiness, strength and skill that has always set the Marines apart. Having highly-trained men and women play an active part-time role in the Marines is more than beneficial to our country. For all an individual gives, they get even more in return: training, good pay, benefits and a chance to bring his or her level of physical and mental fitness to its highest level."

It was that last line that struck a chord with Drew. If he could toughen himself up, he could learn to handle his life better. He knew it wouldn't be easy, that being a Marine Corps reservist wouldn't be that much easier than being a full-time Marine. Reservists still had to undergo the rigors of boot camp, then agree to spend one weekend each month and two weeks each year training with a local Marine Reserve Unit.

"A Reservist is a Marine through and through . . . willing to accept challenges, defend his or her country, and, at all times, be a community leader."

He was sold. If he could be one of the Few, the Proud, the Marines, it would prove he wasn't a worthless bum. *Semper fi*—forever. After talking with the recruiting officer about what the specific duties of a Marine Corps reservist were, Drew signed up.

Although the recruitment material had made it clear that being a reservist was not going to be much easier than being full-time enlistment, for the former Kent State poster boy of partying, boot camp was a revelation.

Being able to survive the initial training was an intense point of pride for Drew, says a friend.

"The Marine Corps, especially in the beginning, was a very tough, hard experience for him. It forced him to grow up and matured him a lot; it was either that or fall apart.

"Just to get through the physical pain of boot camp was a struggle. Drew was in terrible physical shape for a twenty-three-year-old. His idea of exercise was walking across the room to pull another beer out of the refrigerator.

"Drew admits he was soft and often the brunt of the drill instructor. He said he was sometimes the whipping boy that they got down on. But he also ended up getting perfect scores on his physical fitness tests, which just goes to show how hard he worked at it. It absolutely turned his life around."

"I became a functioning human for the first time ever," Carey concurs. "My tour of duty lasted six years, and during that time when I wasn't in uniform, I took college courses and improved my life. It was great."

It also turned him into a gun *aficionado*.

"Yeah, I still own several guns, but I keep them all locked up." Drew says. "I'm a really safe gun owner; the clips are loaded but they are not in the handguns."

Although being a reservist made him feel better about himself and gave him a satisfying sense of accomplishment, Drew was still fairly aimless as far as figuring out what he wanted to do with his life. But at least now he wasn't sitting around idle waiting to find out. When he took college courses, he was a diligent student, determined to get the most out of his classes.

By 1985, Drew was still living in the family home, his mother having left a year earlier to move in with her new husband, George Collinswood. Drew's room was in the basement, near a makeshift wine cellar built by the house's original owner. For some reason, the wine cellar became Drew's monster under the bed.

"My father bought the house in 1958 from an Italian couple who grew grapes in the yard and bottled their own wine," Drew explains. "They built a wine cellar to store wine in, and it's really scary. I hardly ever opened it, even after I grew up."

During those reserve years Carey supported himself by working a series of odd jobs, mostly as a waiter. He took jobs at the local Hilton Hotel, a restaurant downtown called Sammy's and—his favorite—Denny's, where he worked the third shift.

"I liked being a waiter," Drew says with a shrug. "Every day is different. You get to meet really nice people. I like interacting with people. But I am kind of a loner, though, when I choose to be."

In the fall of 1985, Drew's future finally began to take a more definite shape. It started with Carey losing a job. It was far from the first time.

"I was working as a waiter and I got in a big fight with

my boss one time." He laughs. "He was more than my boss—he was the owner of the restaurant. Before I started doing stand-up, I *never* really held any job for over a year.

"So, here I was, without a job again when this friend of mine made me an offer. He was a disc jockey at a Connecticut radio station and he thought I was funny so he said if I ever thought of any jokes for his morning radio show, he'd pay me. Like, you know, ten or twenty bucks, something like that.

"And I thought, *Wow, I can make like a hundred bucks a week off this guy, this chump,* you know? So I went to the downtown Cleveland library and checked out a book on how to write jokes. I think the name of it was *How to Write Comedy* by Brad Ashton. I pored over that book, taking notes and practically memorizing it, and taught myself how to write jokes.

"So I worked at it and in November of 1985, I sent some jokes I had written to him to see if he thought they were funny. That New Year's Eve, I made it my New Year's resolution that in 1986 I was going to go up on the first amateur night of the year at a local comedy club and give it a shot.

"Which I did—and totally bombed. But after that, there was no turning back," says Carey. "I knew this was something I could be good at, so I started going to these amateur nights. And by that April, I got my first job in comedy. I got hired as an emcee and was paid a hundred dollars for the first week, working nine shows and doing about ten minutes each show."

But nothing is ever a straight line with Drew. Although he felt at home onstage and had found a way to make money working with the love of his life, he did his best to sabotage himself.

"Yeah, I quit my show later on in the summer. Actually, I kind of cracked and walked off the floor. It was like a big scene.

"Fuck you, fuck you!

"And I walked away. Then for just about the whole rest of the year, I made no money. I didn't make any money again in comedy until the end of the first year. I remember I had a gig in Pittsburgh at a place called the Funny Bone. I think I was going to get four hundred dollars for the week. And I remember marking it on my calendar going, *Wow, four hundred bucks. I can't wait till that week comes up. I'm going to make four hundred bucks!*"

When Drew decided to brave the stage, he didn't go up with a preconceived gimmick. Preoccupied about bombing and about whether or not he could make the audience laugh, he hadn't given any thought to developing a persona.

"No, I didn't make up this character," Carey says, referring to his now-trademark conservative, white shirt-tie-suit-glasses look. "Everybody thinks this is like something I thought about. As if I sat at home going, *Hmm, now what would be an amusing character for my stage act,* you know?

"What happened was that I was still in the Marine Reserves in '86 when I started doing stand-up comedy and so I already had the buzz cut. And these aren't the original glasses, but if you ever saw anybody in military glasses, they're very similar to this.

"I always wore glasses in the evening. I wore contacts, too, but they were only for daily wear. At night I'd just wear my regular Marine glasses when I went out. I just didn't realize how stupid they looked on me."

He did, however, go for laughs with the suit he originally wore, another example of Carey's misguided fashion sense.

"I had this suit that hung all over me because *Stop Making Sense,* the Talking Heads movie, had come out the year before and I bought a big suit because I thought everybody was going to be wearing them. I looked so stupid in it that I just kept it in my closet. But like, the second amateur night I thought, *I'll just put on this big suit and see what happens.*

"And I just got this big laugh when I walked out onstage. And I thought, *Well . . . okay.* So, for the longest time I thought, *Wow, I just look goofy in my hair and glasses and that's what makes the thing. That's what they're laughing at.*

"Then one time I locked myself out of my bedroom. I was staying in this condo and I accidentally pressed in that little button near the door handle and the door locked when I closed it. I couldn't get into the bedroom to get into the closet where my clothes were and I didn't have time to get a locksmith over to open it for me. So I went to the club and had to go onstage in my regular clothes and my real glasses, the ones that I wore instead of the big black ones.

"When I walked out onstage, people busted up like I was dressed for my other act. I thought, *Holy shit, man, these people are laughing at* me *everywhere I goddamn go,* you know? I couldn't believe it. So I realized I must be like a goofy-looking guy—I just had no idea up until then.

"There's my story, and I'm sticking to it."

FOUR

Drew had finally figured out what he wanted to do with his life. Now all he had to do was get good enough to make a decent living at it; already he was commanding up to $300 a night to perform, when he had work. Actually, Carey's dreams were a little loftier than just becoming a self-supporting, solid stand-up comic. He wanted to be a *great* stand-up comic. In fact, he wanted to be considered one of the best ever. And to that end, he set a goal that would fuel and consume him for the next several years.

"I was going to appear on *The Tonight Show* with Johnny Carson—and be asked to come sit on the couch. I had no doubts I could make that happen."

That dream was what kept Drew going through the countless hours spent on the highways driving from one comedy club to the next. If, as Steve Martin has said, comedy isn't pretty, then life on the road is plain ugly. But traveling the comedy circuit is the rite of passage every stand-up must go through.

"The thing about stand-up," says one comic, "is that you have to keep doing it, and do it fresh, in front of bodies."

There was a more basic reason for going on the road—

the more places you played, the more people who would know your name. Going on the road was still the best way to get known. The rule of thumb among comics is that it takes on average four to seven years of relentless plugging before a stand-up can make a good living, which can be in the $100,000 range, working the top comedy clubs, cruise ships and awards and industrial show circuit.

Comics who have achieved a certain status and income travel from gig to gig by plane. But Carey was still trying to make a name for himself and didn't have the money for such a luxury. Instead, he packed up an old station wagon and hit the road, performing in any comedy club that would have him. He ended up living out of his car for the better part of a year.

"It was a comfy old station wagon—with lots of room," he jokes, before getting serious. "Actually, that was a pretty bad time for me. It was miserable. I was depressed and angry all the time."

Even though he was thrilled to be doing comedy, which had given him a career and a sense of purpose, and to be getting paid for making people laugh, following his ambition meant Drew had to leave behind the woman he had fallen in love with and intended to marry.

Carey met Jacqueline Tough in 1988 while he was still living full-time in Cleveland. Thanks to the deal Drew had made with his mom to rent the family home for $250 a month, he could get by on his still meager earnings. One of the clubs where Drew regularly performed was called the Cleveland Comedy Club. Jackie, then a struggling artist herself, worked there as a waitress and was attracted from afar to Drew's humor and Regular Joe qualities.

"He was just such a nice guy," she says simply.

A nice guy who was also a bit clueless at picking up mating-dance clues. Jackie says that if she had waited for Drew to ask her out, they might have never started dating.

"Drew was so shy, I don't know if he would have ever initiated anything," Jackie told the *Star* in an interview. "I couldn't believe how quiet he was once he got offstage. I actually had to ask *him* out."

But once they finally got to spend some time together, Jackie says, the relationship exploded. Drew was such a romantic that, the way Tough tells it, their courtship became the stuff of clichés.

"It really was love at first sight. We fell in love very quickly. Drew swept me off my feet, and I couldn't have been happier about it."

Drew fell hard. According to pals, Jackie was Drew's first serious, committed, grown-up relationship. He'd always been an emotional loner, but with Jackie he opened up.

"I was really taken with Drew, because he's such a gentleman, so old-fashioned and romantic," said Tough, describing how in the beginning Drew doted on her. "He brought me flowers every chance he got; he'd just show up at home with the biggest bouquet he could afford that day. He's a very giving, generous person."

He was also a generous lover, according to Jackie, who described details of the evening they were first intimate.

"He took me out to dinner and while sitting at the restaurant, he told me how much he loved me. Afterwards we went dancing. Drew loves to dance, and we were out on the floor for hours. By the time we got back to his house, we were all hot and sweaty from dancing, and we never cooled off. One thing led to another, and we became lovers. It was great."

The misty-eyed couple had only gone out on a handful of dates when they decided to live together in Drew's house, which was in less than sparkling condition. After his dad died, it was all Carey's mom could do to feed, clothe and educate her three sons, so the house and furnishings had fallen into disrepair over the years. And Drew didn't have the money to splurge on a new coat of paint or less tattered furniture. It was not exactly the honeymoon house of Jackie's dream; she might have been in love with Drew, but that didn't mean she shared his blind love for the family home.

"I swear the house was straight out of the sixties, like something you'd see in *All in the Family*—except Archie Bunker's house was classier," Jackie says, incredulous. "It had disgusting brown sofas and was really run-down. The next time you watch *The Drew Carey Show*, you'll see the house I lived in with Drew. That's what his house really looked like, except the furniture wasn't as nice."

For someone with such a turbulent emotional past, Drew must have felt as if his life had undergone a magical transformation. Instead of an aimless youth, he had a career he lived and breathed plus a woman he planned to grow old with. Now when he looked at the end of the tunnel he saw light and love and endless possibilities. Las Vegas seemed a lifetime away.

Their first months together floated by, buoyed by the idyll—and best behavior—of beginning romance. Drew worked diligently on his act, ever mindful of his *Tonight Show* destiny. Now that, thanks to Jackie, his private life seemed stable, Drew felt emboldened enough to take the next pivotal step. It was time to leave his Cleveland nest. He'd gone as far as he could locally and needed to establish himself in a more national comedy circuit.

Jackie was game to go along on the adventure. In the spring of 1989, they packed up their belongings in a rental truck and headed west. Los Angeles seemed a logical place to start. Plus, Drew had some friends there who had agreed to put Jackie and him up until they got settled. But like a blind-side hit in the head, their great adventure had turned into a great *mis*adventure by the time they'd crossed the Mississippi.

"It was the trip from hell," Tough says bluntly.

There's an old adage about how taking a vacation together tests the mettle of a relationship, whether it be among family members, friends or couples. There's a unique stress that accompanies traveling by car; individual personality traits and quirks balloon in direct proportion to the length of the trip. By his own admission, Drew is by nature solitary. Although he might have adored Jackie, he also needed a sizable chunk of mental elbow room. Cars, however, are not bastions of personal space. The close quarters made him edgy and uncommunicative.

Mix in Drew's anxiety about leaving home for the great

California unknown and their shaky financial situation and
voilà, you have instant stress in a sedan.

"There was tons of tension," Jackie says. "It was a long,
grueling trip. When we finally arrived in Los Angeles, we
were basically flat broke. We were so poor that we had to
live with one of Drew's friends in their tiny apartment."

Not only were they still on top of one another in forced
proximity, the apartment where they were crashing was
situated in a dreary, unsavory part of Los Angeles—an area
better known as Hollywood. The shiny, possibility-filled
image of Hollywood projected in popular mythology and
media was nowhere to be found. Their introduction to the
City of Angels was of a homeless-ridden, shabby urban
area.

The Hollywood of lore was pretty much an invention,
anyway. At one time, "downtown" Hollywood was a hub,
with restaurants like the Brown Derby and Musso & Franks
catering to the rich and famous. But years ago, the hoi polloi
took over and the more gilded residents moved west to
Beverly Hills, Brentwood, Pacific Palisades and Santa
Monica. Hollywood can be a fun place to visit as a tourist
but, although it's undergone some gentrification in recent
years, it can be a disheartening place to live for a new
transplant. When the tourist places close down for the night,
hookers, drug pushers, runaways and the homeless take over
the streets. Walking around at night is not the wisest choice
for the survival-minded. But driving around in a car can
exacerbate feelings of isolation that the sheer size and
unique layout of L.A. tend to create.

L.A.'s car culture was born out of necessity. Instead of
one central business area, Los Angeles is spread out in
distinct communities that are linked by more miles of roads
and freeways than probably any other American city. For
transplants coming from the main urban areas east of the
Mississippi, the fundamental difference in lifestyle de-
manded by the city's physical layout can be hard to adapt to.
For Drew, it was almost physically painful, and it actually
angered him. Even after he established himself in the L.A.
comedy clubs, he harbored unrelenting ill will toward L.A.

He incorporates this animosity into his act, directed mostly
at the inconsistency between "Hollywood's" glitzy, glamorous image and its occasionally dreary reality—the streets
routinely populated by homeless, drunks and hookers.

"I feel bad for the homeless, but in Hollywood, on the
streets, most of those guys are just mean drunks. Those are
the guys I can't stand."

"Gimme a dollar."

*"No, get away from me! I'm not gonna give you a dollar,
asshole.* Earn *a dollar. Jump up and down, let me see what
you can do."*

Of course, ten minutes from the main business section of
Hollywood are numerous residential neighborhoods with
palm tree–lined streets and parks and coffeehouses and
corner shops. But Drew's lack of resources prevented him
from moving out of Hollywood's leaner, meaner streets.

But despite the distaste he had for L.A., even Carey had
to admit it was fun to see movie stars at the local gas station.

"The one good thing about living in L.A. is that you get
to see a lot of celebrities. And I'm still starstruck seeing
stars. I saw Sally Struthers walking down the street. That
was kind of cool. I dunno"—he gives a wicked smile—"I
gave her a dollar."

One positive consequence of his L.A. hostility was that it
spurred Carey to be even more dogged in his ambition to
become one of the great comics. One didn't have to worry
about Drew wasting a lot of time lolling at the beach or
hanging out in West Hollywood's fashionable outdoor cafés.

Drew's dedication to his stand-up career had yielded
fairly quick results. In 1987, he had auditioned for and was
chosen to be a contestant on *Star Search.* He made two
appearances on the TV talent show. His first outing, Carey
received four stars and was invited back to compete again.
But the second time, he lost. The comedian who beat him
out? Who knows?

When asked if he is bitter about losing to someone who
went on to anonymity, Carey laughs.

"You betcha," he shoots back. "But ya know, I've decided
it's never good to win *Star Search.* Yeah, think about it.

Sinbad lost. Dennis Miller lost. I lost. Jenny Jones is the only one who was a winner on *Star Search* that I know who's done anything—and look at her. Case closed, I say."

Sinbad agrees that winning amateur talent contests is overrated.

"I remember being at some comedy festival where Eddie Murphy finished second or third behind I don't even *remember* who. I don't think it hurt *his* career. When they were getting ready to cast *48 Hrs*. I doubt they went, *Hmm, should we star him or that other guy who won the festival?*"

When Carey first walked into the famous comedy club the Improv, he faced the daunting task of not only following in some serious comedy footsteps, but he also had to prove himself to the reigning stand-up kings of the L.A. club scene. According to an Improv regular, the top comics at any given time are a cliquish bunch who see themselves as breathing rarefied air.

"They set themselves apart from the less successful comic, like a comedy Rat Pack," says a longtime Improv worker. "It's like they've got a transparent curtain around them. They're nice to new people to the extent they will compliment your show, but it's real clear you are not one of them. They don't readily befriend newcomers. Drew had a particularly tough time being accepted as one of the top comedians with these guys.

"There's this one big round table at the Improv and guys like Larry Miller and Jerry Seinfeld and Paul Reiser and Bill Maher and Richard Belzer would sit at this table with Improv owner Budd Friedman. They'd either sit there waiting to go up and try out some material or they'd be there checking out somebody else's act. But when they sit there, you definitely sense that they see themselves as the top dogs."

Then you have Drew.

"I remember when he first came to L.A. and would work the Improv," says a friend. "He was the very essence of the outsider. Even after people got to know him, he still had an aura of being a loner. It's ironic, because his act was so funny that he got a lot of attention from people wanting to be friends, but he's very independent."

Part of Drew's apparent distance might have been an outgrowth of his personal "bullshit detector," says the friend.

"He's one of a group of comics around now, like Jim Carrey, Rosie O'Donnell and Denis Leary, who have made careers out of popping the balloons of people who are a bit too full of themselves. He loves to punch holes in pretentiousness.

"With people like Bill Maher, for example, everything is image," says the friend, speaking about the host of ABC's late-night *Politically Incorrect*. Maher's reputation for being a diva was heightened after it was reported he had stormed out of a trendy restaurant in a huff because the owner wouldn't immediately seat him and his entourage of eight—without reservations.

"That's the reputation he's got. And of course with Drew, everything is anti-image. Someone acting like they're too important would be laughed at by people in Drew's old neighborhood. There was a code there: You do not put on airs. He's the original anti-airs guy, to the extent that he makes no apologies for being overweight and still gets his hair cut by the same barber, a former Marine who runs a little shop in Hollywood.

"But being down-to-earth is part of Drew's life and credo. It's what keeps him grounded regardless of what craziness is going on around him. When he's on the road and needs his hair cut, he looks around for a barber near a military base, partly because they know how to do the kind of military cut he likes but also because being around that atmosphere keeps him close to his Marine roots.

"The dark side of Drew Carey is that, at least in his early days in L.A., he realized he had a slim enough emotional grasp of things that he needed to continually ground himself. Most people can change without fear of losing who they are. Most people can go, *I can move on now*. But he does not want to do that."

Nobody can accuse Carey of falling under L.A.'s spell and going Hollywood. His suit-and-tie "uniform" had already become a performance trademark by the time he got to L.A., but it was also a badge of individuality.

"Yeah, dressing and acting differently from other people who are in comedy and show business is his way of defining himself," says another friend. "And when he first came to L.A., he wore that suit like armor. Even when he wasn't performing, anytime he'd come to the Improv, he'd have on that suit and tie."

One of the perks of working at Friedman's club was that performers got 50 percent off the price of their meals and were allowed to run tabs. Not surprisingly, the club was a haven for hungry comics, including Drew, who became a regular at the Improv.

"But where most comics would hang out and socialize, Drew was always seen as an outsider. He wasn't mean or anything, he just didn't seem interested in being part of the crowd. Several times he'd come to the club with Jackie and for the most part, they'd just be off by themselves."

Other friends say Drew simply didn't want anything to distract him from the reason he had come to L.A. in the first place   to be the greatest stand-up comic of his generation.

In the fall of 1989, Drew was feeling antsy. He needed to get out there again, to subject himself to the grind of road warrior stand-up. It's the way comics get razor-sharp, how they learn to hone their timing and other skills and to milk good crowds and, more important, turn around bad ones. So Drew packed up his old station wagon, kissed Jackie good-bye and drove off. Carey's time away from Jackie was a miserable experience, no doubt made worse because he was living like a vagabond out of his car, returning to L.A. periodically only to regroup before heading out again. And it was no easier for Jackie being the one left behind.

"It was terrible, because he was never, never around," she recalls. "When he *was* home, we'd spend all of our time just trying to catch up and get on equal footing again."

Although Carey believed that his troubles with Jackie

stemmed mostly from his long and continued absences, she admits their problems went much deeper. Drew's tendency to bury his feelings created a wedge Jackie couldn't bridge.

"It was very hard to communicate with Drew," Jackie says. "We never really talked. That was our biggest problem, and that's what eventually tore us apart."

Years later, Drew admitted that he's not someone who easily opens up. He's much more comfortable not delving too deeply into his psyche, which helps explain why he didn't seek the help of a psychiatrist after his suicide attempts.

"I'm not that introspective," he says. "I only like to look to the future."

Suddenly, Drew's future was looking much more solitary. He and Jackie had been together for about a year and had struggled against a variety of obstacles. They had been buffeted by financial difficulties, relocated to a new city, been culture-shocked by a significantly different lifestyle— all while trying to adjust to the pressures and stresses of learning to live with a lover. With Drew either unwilling or unable to open up to Jackie and communicate to her the way she needed him to, the relationship imploded.

"Drew didn't take the breakup very well." Jackie sighs. "He cried and begged me not to leave him. But the relationship just wasn't working, and I knew it. I'd had enough; it was time to end it."

For several months, Drew refused to believe it was really over.

"He was really devastated, and kept trying to change my mind," she recalls. "He called constantly and told me how much he loved me. But I knew it was a hopeless situation."

Friends say they have no doubt Drew and Jackie genuinely cared for each other, but they were too different. In a *TV Guide* interview, Drew talked about his idea of a fantasy vacation:

"Driving across country by myself. Then I have solitude. I'm very much a loner. I don't need to have anyone else around. I can entertain myself by reading or watching TV. I can even just think of stuff in my own head to keep me interested. I really like being alone."

One of the passions he indulges in while alone is music.

"I like to listen to all kinds of music. I listen to country and rap and I even love heavy metal. I'm pretty much open to anything—Snoop Doggy Dogg, Pearl Jam, Garth Brooks. I get bored real easy with stuff, so I won't listen to just one type of music."

In thinking what might have been with Jackie, Carey adds:

"If I had a wife, I'd have to have my own office, where I could disappear. Or separate homes. Sometimes, I hear an actor complain that he doesn't live in the same city as his wife and I think, *Yeah! Where do I sign up for that?*"

Then Carey makes a curious juxtaposition.

"You know, both times that I tried to kill myself, I had ambivalent feelings. *Uh-oh—is this really the right thing?* It's like being at the altar, I guess. Suicide equals marriage."

Someone with two suicide attempts in his hip pocket might have been expected to go off the deep end after getting dumped. But Drew didn't. He was hurt and angry— but in a healthy way. It was a comforting testament to just how far he'd come since hitting bottom in Las Vegas. When asked if he's ever thought about suicide again, Carey is definite.

"No, no, no. That's all over."

Jackie agrees.

"Drew has spent more time than anybody I know reading and listening to tapes on positive thinking and pop psychology. He has taken all these ingredients and made his own soup out of them. He really does have a positive outlook. Nothing's going to change that."

A couple of years later, as Drew's career was really taking off, he and Jackie got back together, hoping to rekindle their romance. They discovered that it hadn't been just outside obstacles that had driven them apart.

"As soon as we got back with each other, the same old problems came back, too, so we didn't stay together long. But after a while we started talking, and now I consider Drew one of my closest friends. I couldn't be happier with how things have turned out for him. He's got a Top 10 series, has been able to buy his dream home in Beverly Hills and is dating lots of beautiful young ladies. He's a good guy, and I wish him nothing but the best in his life."

FIVE

Although Carey described his road life as miserable, it wasn't without its lighter moments. As he got to know other comics traveling the same circuit, he managed to forge a few friendships. Even the normally reticent Drew needed company on occasion. One of his road buddies was an aspiring Chicago stand-up named John Caponera who, in the early part of his career, was known for his impressions.

"My senior year in college, I had to do a monologue for an Advanced Public Speaking course final exam. A lot of the kids were doing stuff off of Richard Pryor albums and whatnot. I said, *The hell with that, I'm just going to do my own thing*. I put together this Hollywood celebrity baseball game; it was a bunch of impressions of famous guys playing baseball.

"So I do this bit and it goes over great in class and I get an A for the course. Then about a week later, some kid comes up and tells me they're doing a local *Gong Show* in Joliet. I said, 'What the hell are you telling *me* for?' And he suggests I go and do the bit from class and I say, 'I'm not a stand-up!' But he says I should do it anyway. So I did—and won five hundred dollars.

"Then a month later I went to another bar after playing some softball and *they* were holding their own mock *Gong Show*. So, I did the bit again and won another five hundred dollars.

"So I figured, *Hey, maybe I got something as a stand-up*," Caponera says, then jokes, "I'm doing that same stupid act to this day.

"No, the truth is, after a year I was sick of it. I didn't want to be known as an impressionist because then you become a novelty act and start working cruise ships. I said, *Down with that*. So I tossed all the impressions away and worked on a stand-up act."

By the time Drew met John, Caponera was better known and on a slightly faster career track than he was. But they became friends and John enjoyed hanging out with Drew. They spent a lot of time together, often appearing at the same clubs.

"We played poker together a bunch of times and just hung out," says Drew.

"They were road warriors together, and that creates a special kind of bond between comics," adds a friend, "They would go out and party together, although Drew can outparty almost anyone. They shared a lot of wild times together, especially in Texas."

Texas made a particular impression on Drew. While he might not have enjoyed life on the Texas byroads, the experience at least provided him with new material.

One of Carey's strengths is his way of making everyday things that the rest of us, or at least Texans, take for granted suddenly look ridiculous, such as drive-through liquor stores, where people can pull up to a window on the side of the store and buy whatever booze you desire. Mind you, while driving.

"It's almost a good idea; just the thing for that drunk driver on the go."

"*Hey, no time to stop at a real bar, got things to do today. Places to go, people to hit.*"

"At Christmastime: '*Up on the sidewalk, thump, thump, thump.*'"

It's a case of the pot calling the kettle drunk. Carey had never lost the love of drinking that he had developed at Kent State. He was still a serious beer drinker and occasionally he got out of hand, like a rowdy teenage boy.

"John Caponera loves to tell about the time he and Drew were in some backwater Texas town on the Gulf Coast," says a buddy. "They rented a convertible one night and were just driving around, drinking some beers and hanging out.

"Apparently, Drew had one beer too many, and he told John to drive down this restricted roadway that led to the beach. You know that scene you see in movies where people drive down the beach in a convertible and someone is either standing up in the seat or sitting on the back hood? Well, that's what Drew wanted to do.

"Drew stood up in the car and was yelling for John to drive to the beach—but John wouldn't do it. The last thing he wanted was to get busted by some Texas Ranger. But it was nights like that that cemented their friendship. That, and trying to teach Drew to play golf."

According to the friend, Caponera was never threatened by or jealous of Drew's obvious talent.

"John is a real laid-back kind of guy. He liked Drew and even helped him get a lot of jobs. In the beginning, when they performed together, John would be the closer, meaning he went on last. Clubs usually had three comics perform a night. Drew would be the middle act and John would be last. The idea is to save your best for the final set. But as Drew got better and better, it got harder and harder for John to close Drew. Some comics would have let their egos get in the way and held it against Drew, but that's not the kind of guy he is."

In fact, a few years down the road, Caponera would play a huge part in helping Drew break into the television viewing public's eye. But as the 1990s neared, Drew was merely dreaming of not having to live out of his car anymore. Then came a setback that might have demoralized anyone else—Drew missed a call from *The Tonight Show*. A friend explains what happened.

"When Drew wasn't on the road, he was knocking

himself out playing the L.A. clubs, knowing that was the way *The Tonight Show*'s talent bookers would find him— that, and word of mouth about what comic was currently hot. And the thing is, Drew got a lot of really good word of mouth almost as soon as he got to town."

Like most other performers, Drew had an answering service that he checked in with regularly. It was his lifeline to jobs.

"Then Drew went out of town, I believe to visit Jackie, who he was trying to get back together with," recalls the friend. "And he went for a couple days without bothering to check his service. When he finally did call for messages, there was a call from *The Tonight Show* booker saying they wanted him on the show. But they had only given him like twenty-four hours' notice and said they needed to know his availability immediately.

"Drew called back and told them yes, he was available that night. But the booker told him that since he hadn't called back, they'd gotten someone else. They told Drew, 'We'll get back to you.'"

Carey wouldn't hear from *The Tonight Show* for two more years.

Instead of disheartening Drew or undermining his resolve, the lost opportunity had the surprising effect of bolstering his determination. He chose to see the missed chance as a blessing—the next time the show called, his act would be that much better. He'd *kill*.

In the meantime, he kept working. He spent his days writing and thinking up new bits. One of his most successful was the "X-ray Specs" routine, in which Drew uses his industrial-strength eyeglasses to see through women's clothes. Carey says the idea literally just popped into his head.

"One day I was getting dressed in front of the mirror and it just occurred to me, to tell you the truth." He laughs. "That's all there was to it. There was no great creative process involved.

"I went like that in front of the mirror and it cracked me up, so I did it onstage that night. I have a lonely home life."

He chuckles. "I spend a lot of hours in front of the mirror trying out things with my own body."

X-ray Specs was an instant hit with audiences. One comic describes the bit as funny, but juvenile.

"Yeah, it's a very childish gag, like a twelve-year-old. But that's part of Drew's appeal. You have to remember, at least with guys, there's a difference between those guys who could get the cool girls in high school and those who couldn't, like Drew. It's a real thing for a guy when he feels like a reject as a teenager. It really can stay with you to some degree throughout your life; somewhere deep inside you see yourself as the nerd girls wouldn't look twice at.

"Obviously, Drew is now a TV star and popular and has lots of women around him, but he still exudes the remnants of someone who's suffered a lot of rejection. And that's part of what makes the X-ray Specs bit so funny. It's kind of like the nerd's revenge."

In other words, Carey takes the very things that caused him to feel like an outsider and loner and uses them to his advantage.

"A good contrast with Drew is Jim Carrey," says a comedy club regular. "Jim's act is, *Oh, you love me. I'm going to be goofy and you're going to love me for it and I'll love you back.* It's a silly, playful approach.

"But with Drew, his underlying approach is, *Okay, you're never going to love me, I know that. So fuck you—but I'm going to make you laugh anyway, goddamnit, you fuckers. In spite of how you really feel about me, I'll make you laugh, in spite of yourself.*

"That's why much of his act is about needling other people's ideas and taking them to task. Above all else, though, Drew loves to do stuff to piss people off. He loves that; he lives for that."

When Drew is performing, there's an obvious nervous energy driving him. He paces the stage, eyes darting, firing off lines in bursts. Although he is always smiling and often laughs at his own jokes, there's also an edginess to him.

"Oh, yeah," agrees a friend. "He still has the devil inside him. Watch him closely when he performs and there's an edge just below the surface. There's never a relaxed performance from Drew."

The more Carey warms up to a subject, the faster his delivery. A favorite target are animal rights groups, which he makes clear get on his nerves.

"The big thing I've noticed lately is dolphin-safe tuna. That's great—if you're a dolphin. But what if you're a tuna? There's probably some tuna floppin' around in a ship somewhere going:

"Hey, what about me, son of a bitch?"

Nothing—and nobody—is safe from Drew's acerbic observations.

"Have you seen those ads Sally Struthers has for that correspondence school? Pathetic, isn't it? That's when I knew she'd hit the skids, you know?"

One advantage of Carey's rumpled stage persona was that it didn't cost a lot to keep up his wardrobe.

"All my shirts are from Kmart; yep, that's where I get 'em," he said somewhat proudly during a 1994 interview. "They're all Catch brand. I just buy them in threes, you know, and take 'em home. I have something like ten or twelve of these. And then I've got some older ones that have been washed so much they're all beat up so I have to buy ten to replace those.

"I always go to Kmart, even though they shrink because they are cheaply made . . . Then I have to go buy new ones, but I don't throw the shrunken ones out because I always think I'm going to lose weight and I'll be able to fit into them. So I have all these shirts that I'm too fucking fat for that hopefully I'll be able to get into someday."

For a comedian, so much is riding on establishing a unique act that Carey was understandably dismayed to discover that there was another comic on the circuit with a nearly identical stage persona named Brian Haley. They were similar enough that Drew says he would frequently get mistaken for Haley.

"The first time I met Brian was at the Holy City Zoo up in San Francisco," Drew recalls. "It was this really tiny comedy club and they used to hire, like, three comics who would take turns headlining. And they'd switch the order around all week.

"Sometimes I'd go on first and Brian would have to follow me, then other times I'd have to go on right after Brian. And here we were, both wearing old suits with skinny ties. I mean, we could have been twins. He had been in the Green Berets and I had been in the Marines and we both wore our hair in buzz cuts.

"I thought I had thought it up all on my own and here this guy was. The only difference was he didn't wear glasses. It was really scary. People would come up and compliment me on a bit that was Brian's. *Oh, I think you're so funny*. It was really strange."

But the confusion wouldn't last much longer. In November of 1991, *The Tonight Show* called again, and this time Carey was ready. The gig would turn out to be not just the realization of a long-standing goal, but the starting point of a new phase of his career.

"Without a doubt, Drew's appearance on *The Tonight Show* was a springboard," says a friend. "It literally changed his life and career."

When Johnny Carson was hosting *The Tonight Show*, it was the Mecca for any stand-up. An appearance could literally make a career. At the very least, it virtually guaranteed invitations to other shows and bigger bookings nationwide. The ultimate compliment and affirmation sought after by every stand-up who appeared on the show was to be invited to come sit on the couch to talk with Carson. It was not a rehearsed thing. It really was like performing in front of the King. If he liked the act, you were summoned. Otherwise, the camera would show him applauding, then there would be a quick cut to commercial.

The pressure comics felt to please Carson caused some to choke and others to shine. Ellen DeGeneres was the first female stand-up in the first twenty-four years of Carson's reign to be asked over to the couch. That appearance ultimately launched her cable and network television career. Drew was hoping for a similar miracle.

He got it. He gave one of the performances of his career, and in reward Carson gave Drew the ultimate compliment—he waved him over and invited him to sit down next to him. A lot of stand-ups, when summoned to the couch, would be visibly nervous. Without the shield of their routine, some of the comics came across as tongue-tied and somewhat dull. Not Carey. This was the moment he had been working for. He was going to enjoy it and make the most of it. He not only chatted comfortably with Johnny, but he also joked with Ed McMahon about his lack of success on *Star Search*.

"You feel regal. It was like being anointed a knight, like walking into show business with the red carpet. But then once you're there for a minute or so, you start noticing, *Wow, this is really shitty furniture. How does it look so good on TV?*"

In testimony to just how impressed Carson was with Carey then and later, part of that performance is included in the *Best of Carson* home video.

"I would take a bullet for Johnny Carson," Carey says now, acknowledging the contribution the King of Late Night made to his career. "That man is God, I tell you."

Soon after his *Tonight Show* appearance, Drew found himself in a career whirlwind. Suddenly, he was getting offers from places like Showtime. He wrote and starred in two comedy specials for the cable giant, *Full Frontal Comedy* and *Drew Carey, Human Cartoon*, for which he won a Cable Ace Award. In 1993 he was also nominated for another Cable Ace Award for his performance in the *Tenth Anniversary of the Montreal Comedy Festival* special. Suddenly, he was all over television in shows like HBO's *14th Annual Young Comedians Show* and *Comic Strip Live* and MTV's *½ Hour Comedy Hour, Comics Only* and *Hot Country Nights*.

Now instead of playing small Texas clubs, Carey was the opening act for Jermaine Jackson and the Marshall Tucker Band at big arenas, and he also played in Las Vegas. Returning to the scene of his nearly self-inflicted crime was a personal triumph. It seemed unreal that only a little more than ten years earlier he had been so hopeless that he had wanted to die. It convinced Drew that the best therapy was discipline, hard work and a positive outlook.

That recipe would continue to serve him well in reaching his next goal—Drew had decided to conquer prime time. Carey wanted to join the ranks of Reiser, Seinfeld, Ellen DeGeneres and Brett Butler: stand-ups who had their own popular sitcoms.

Among the L.A. comedy club hierarchy the Comedy Store and the Improv are the elite venues because both have histories of—or at least take credit for—helping to launch dozens of careers. Jay Leno, Robin Williams, Pauly Shore, David Letterman, Larry Miller and many others are alumni of the two clubs, and it's no coincidence that most of them have ended up on their own television shows.

Casting agents and producers regularly scout for new talent at the Improv and the Comedy Store. And in recent years, most new sitcoms are built around the stand-up flavor of the moment. But harvesting comedy club talent is as old as television itself. Comics, long a mainstay in radio, crossed over to the then-new medium of television in 1948; at the time, there were only a couple hundred thousand sets in the country. NBC took a chance and hired a radio comedian named Milton Berle to host a new variety show called *Texaco Star Theater*. Ever since then, networks have drawn from the stand-up ranks for sitcoms and variety shows developed to showcase a comic's particular talents.

Comic John Caponera believes it makes perfect sense that network producers look to the comedy clubs for series inspiration.

"I think it's a natural transition for stand-ups to go into sitcoms. As a comic, you're up onstage and constantly delivering a line. You *know* how to deliver a line. You have timing. And you learn those things through years of doing stand-up.

"I think the reason stand-ups go from club work to situation comedy television series is because their characters have been finely honed over the years. They're recognized and identifiable by the public.

"So instead of trying to come up with a sitcom character from scratch, they go to a comic who already has the character developed. Then all they have to do is put him in the right vehicle so he can shine."

Carey, who hates overanalysis of any kind, has a simpler take on it.

"We go into sitcoms, man, because we're *funny*."

SIX

In 1994, NBC had yet to coin the line "Must See TV." That's because the network was still in the process of rebuilding lost glory. When *The Cosby Show* was king of the Nielsen Ratings hill, the Peacock was the number one network. Invariably, though, a network's fortunes will ebb and flow, because the nature of prime-time television superiority is cyclical, and after *Cosby* and some other popular shows went off the air, hard times hit the network.

Ironically, it is reaction to success that usually causes the downfall. A network languishing behind the leader has more incentive to take programming risks, to give unheralded performers a chance they might not otherwise get. The top network of the moment tends to play it safe, not wanting to rock the boat by being too innovative.

There is a good reason for the tendency of the upper-echelon brass to avoid risk-taking: While the rewards can be great, there can also be tremendous failure. Remember *Cop Rock*? ABC broke new ground by putting a musical on its schedule. It might have also broken a record for the most scathing reviews ever received by a television show. While some critics and viewers thought it *was* innovative, the much-hyped series was a flop. At the same time, ABC's faith in *thirtysomething* resulted in awards, rabid fan loyalty and critical acclaim. *Married . . . with Children* would have been summarily rejected by the "Big Three" networks, but since Fox had nothing to lose, it gave the raunchy comedy a chance. Eleven years later, it became the longest-running sitcom in television history.

Even if it doesn't want to play it safe, a network will stay with a successful show like *Coach* or *Wings* until it runs its course, despite declining ratings. That's when the headaches start. Suddenly, a network will find itself with a bunch of once-powerful, aging shows ready to retire at the same time. It's like a sports team that finds itself having to start rookies in place of the now-retired All-Stars. There might be talent there, but they haven't won over the fans yet. And with the increased competition among upstart networks and cable, it's harder than ever to launch a breakout hit series— especially dramas, which historically take longer to estab-lish an audience.

So in recent years, the networks have had to rely more and more on half-hour sitcoms to fill out their prime-time schedules. One reason is due to the proliferation of news-magazines taking up time slots that would otherwise be filled by dramas. The other factor is the "recyclability" of sitcoms. Comedy shows do well as season repeats and as summer reruns. Dramas historically don't. That means sitcoms tend to get higher ratings when aired a second and third time, meaning the network makes more advertising money. The fact that dramas take longer to hook regular viewers and that they usually cost more because they are on the air twice as long are other reasons for sitcoms' high profile.

With networks so dependent on situation comedies, it makes sense they spend a sizable portion of their develop-ment money creating starring vehicles for established com-ics. But being a successful stand-up is no guarantee you'll find ratings success on television. Lisa Walters, John Mendoza, Margaret Cho, Dana Carvey, Paula Poundstone and even George Carlin have suffered inglorious flops.

Nor do networks necessarily need stand-ups to create a successful sitcom. Two of the highest-rated comedies in recent years have been *Friends* and *Suddenly Susan*, neither of which stars seasoned stand-ups. But as John Caponera noted, networks still like the advantage identifiable comics offer—an audience who already knows them. Caponera knows, because in 1994 NBC gave him the chance to star in his own series.

The Good Life had a solid pedigree. The series was created by Emmy Award–winning producers/writers Jeff Martin and Kevin Curran, who had worked on *Late Show with David Letterman, Married . . . with Children* and *The Simpsons* before being offered the opportunity to run their own show.

In the beginning, *The Good Life* seemed destined to be, if not a hit, then a solid performer for NBC. The producers were used to success and, when they started putting the show together, had no reason to think *The Good Life* would be any different. Everything was falling into place the way they envisioned it would.

"It was really a smooth process," says Martin. "There weren't a whole lot of twists and turns to it. The network wanted to develop shows for Disney and said they had this guy, John Caponera, under contract. We went, saw his act and said, *Yeah, that guy's funny*. People will say he looks like Al Bundy," Martin jokes, referring to the *Married . . . with Children* character, "but he's funny so that's okay."

Martin says that he and Curran spent the following two weeks trying to figure out how to build a show around John.

"Then Disney said, 'We've got this other guy, Drew Carey, who might be good on the show,'" says Curran. "We saw Drew's *Tonight Show* tape, which is one of the greatest things I've ever seen. He just killed. I tell you, it was an epiphany."

Based on that performance, Curran and Martin agreed to meet with Carey. They recall that when they got Drew and John in the same room, the chemistry was terrific.

"I just thought you'd believe they were pals. You could believe they'd have a rapport; one seems a little more grouchy and one is more easygoing and silly and they had a nice physical balance."

"That means John's slim and I'm fat—that's 'a nice physical balance,'" Drew says snidely. "Thanks, you son of a bitch."

And Caponera and Carey had the same manager, so it was hardly surprising that Drew was hired on to play John's office sidekick, although Jeff Martin says it was Drew's presence and the chemistry between the two comics that sealed the deal.

This was Carey's second brush with a television series. A short while before, he had hooked up with Disney and writer-producer Michael Jacobs for a proposed pilot called *Akron Man.*

"And I'll be glad to send anybody the script if they want to see a sample of Mr. Jacobs's quality writing," Drew says dryly.

But *The Good Life* seemed to be a better situation. Drew liked the producers and felt the studio and network would be behind the series. If he was going to do a series, this was the way to get his foot in the door: with experienced producers, as a supporting player so that the responsibility wasn't on his shoulders and for a company like Disney with a good track record.

Carey is the first to admit he's no actor. But his lack of self-consciousness in front of the camera plays well in sitcom land. By not trying to "act" and just relying on his comedy instincts, Carey avoids the stilted performance of someone playing beyond his capabilities.

Stand-ups who do character pieces in their act, like Billy Crystal, Robin Williams and Whoopi Goldberg, usually have the easiest time making the leap to acting. Those who are more or less "themselves" onstage usually have a more difficult time. For example, no matter what role she plays, Roseanne is essentially Roseanne. Tim Allen puts it in perspective:

"Dialogue people might not think is particularly funny when read becomes funny when I do it. I can be funny all the time as a result of my training, whereas actors can't necessarily.

"However, I can't do *Death of a Salesman*. That's the trade-off."

Drew went into *The Good Life* with the intention of learning the business of television and becoming accustomed to performing in a three-camera format. But what's the point of acting if you can't inject a little fantasy at the same time. One of Drew's suggestions was that it would be funny if his character was the one who got all the ladies.

"Yeah, that was my idea," says Drew, laughing. "I only thought of it because I thought it would be a great scam to meet beautiful actresses and models and stuff. And what do you know—they bought it!

"Unfortunately, though, it didn't spill over into my own life. But at least I got to hang out with them during rehearsals, so that was a good thing."

In *The Good Life,* Caponera played John Bowman, a middle-class, married suburbanite stiff with three children—an elder slacker son, a go-getter daughter and an ultraobedient younger son.

"Yeah, in the pilot they described him as more dog than boy," Carey jokes.

"The show was set in the Chicago area at the Honest Abe Security Company. We worked at a company that manufactured and distributed locks. They picked Chicago because that's where John's from. And they picked the security company because they were looking to have our characters in the most boring job they could find and that's the one that came to mind."

Caponera saw Bowman as a frustrated comic who liked to think that if he hadn't gotten married and had kids early, he might have pursued a career in stand-up.

"He was the kind of guy who liked to be the life of the party but then worried that people were laughing at him instead of with him. In other words, he was the guy I'd probably be if I hadn't gone into comedy," admits Caponera.

"To me, when I watch the show, it's like I'm tuning in on

someone's life, as opposed to watching a sitcom where you got a *ba-ba-boom* joke every ten seconds. You know, I really feel like you're in a day in the life of John Bowman and his friends and his family," Caponera said in one interview.

After listening to Caponera's sincere sentiment, Carey waited a beat, then said, "See, I feel just the opposite: I feel like I'm watching a sitcom."

The press loved him from that minute on.

Balancing Bowman's obnoxiousness and angst was Carey's character, who didn't suffer the pangs that come with worrying all that much about what might have been. He was too busy scoring dates with beautiful babes.

Where John's character was somewhat trapped in his job and family life, Drew's didn't let his nowhere job stop him from larger-than-life living. He was an amateur horticulturist, a world traveler and a Deadhead who'd seen the band in concert eighty-seven times. On paper it might have sounded too silly, but Drew made it seem believable, as far as sitcoms go.

Even though the series was meant to be a showcase for Caponera, Drew wasn't your average second banana. The series also starred Eve Gordan and Monty Hoffman, but they ended up background noise whenever Carey was around. He was just too creative and too funny not to be used. One of his ideas was a set piece at the end of the show, which gave Drew a chance to be spotlighted, although the plan was to rotate the set piece among the cast. Carey was also the one who came up with the title.

"They were coming up with these really bad names, so I thought I'd give it a shot," Carey recalls. "When they said, *Yeah, we like it, let's go with that,* I asked some studio executive if I got anything for coming up with the title. So they set me up with a free hotel room in Vegas."

The only danger of his behind-the-scenes creative involvement was that it might have caused resentment among the other talent, specifically Caponera. It's a common behind-the-scenes problem.

Some series stars have been known to count the number

of jokes written, throw tantrums or walk off sets when a costar starts upstaging them. Take *Cybill*. Even though Christine Baranski and Cybill Shepherd have publicly denied any professional or personal animosity, people close to the set tell another story.

"The short version is that Cybill doesn't want to be upstaged by Christine all the time," says a source. "Christine is the one usually singled out in reviews, Christine is the one who got the Emmy—of course, that's basically because Christine is a damn talented actress. But we're talking ego here, not logic. So there are 'discussions,' that anywhere else would be called arguments, about things like whether Christine is getting too many funny lines.

"It's a double-edged sword. On one hand, Cybill knows that Christine is a big part of the show's success. At the same time, the series *is* called *Cybill*."

But Caponera was the opposite. It had taken him fourteen years to get his shot at prime time, and his number one goal was to have a successful show. He was willing to share the spotlight if that's what it took to have a hit series, so he encouraged Drew's ideas and input. Nor was Carey shy about making suggestions. He knew this was a golden opportunity to learn the ins and outs of the sitcom process. It was also his first real interaction with the television press, an opportunity he enthusiastically embraced.

Facing the press can be a daunting task, especially during press tours, where a couple of hundred journalists gather to hold a panel Q&A session. It's no surprise that stand-ups usually fare well in this setup, because they are used to "handling" a crowd. Carey's humor and blunt honesty made him an instant favorite of journalists tired of hearing carefully coached answers.

One thing Drew can always be counted on is his work ethic. He understands that promotion is as much a part of television as scriptwriting. And he was tireless in his commitment, no matter the hassle. In order to get to *The Good Life*'s press conference, Carey defied distance, weather and airline schedules to arrive there in time.

•   •   •

"First of all, I got bumped from *Letterman* on that Monday, so they had to fly me back to do the makeup appearance, which was a day before the press conference, so that was one thing," Drew recalls.

"I was in Nashville, where I was doing a *Hot Country Jam* special for Dick Clark. So after I finished that, I had to fly to New York that same day. I had like an hour once I landed in New York, so I rushed to the *Letterman* show. Did the *Letterman* show. I got my bags all packed at the *Letterman* show to go straight to the airport. But then they tell me my flight's canceled."

"We called New York and told Drew to forget it and just stay in New York," producer Martin says.

"But I said not while my show needs me," Carey says in his best Marine voice. "So I do the show. When I walk offstage, I get a call from a secretary and she tells me she had an eight o'clock flight for me leaving from La Guardia.

"I got the limo driver and told him we had to get to La Guardia. We threw my stuff into the car. We rushed through the slush. Finally get to La Guardia. I check in really quick. I run to the gate. I get on the plane, like, *Phew, I'm here.*

"And then the plane is delayed for two hours while they deice it. So I miss my connection in Atlanta. I have to go to a La Quinta Inn for four hours. I got four hours to kill. So I just stayed up all night in a Denny's drinking coffee.

"I get to the airport. I fall asleep. *That* plane is late. I have fifteen minutes in Dallas to make my connection to get here. I make my connection. I sleep again on the way here. I get in the limo. I change clothes in the limo on the way over. I mean pants and everything; I'm just ripping off my clothes. We get here. I grab my shirt and iron and I go in. I fill up my iron with water. I end up ironing my shirt in the men's room, and here I am.

"I feel like Jack Lemmon in *The Out-of-Towners*. There's the story. Yeah, it was an ordeal. You cannot believe what I went through to get here. And this is it? Holy shit! I could be sleeping at the Rihga Royal right now," he says, referring to the New York hotel the *Letterman* show would have put him up in.

The Good Life was readied to go on as a mid-season replacement in January 1994. The first sign that perhaps the fates weren't smiling on the show was the time slot NBC gave it: Tuesdays at 8:30, opposite an ABC comedy juggernaut led by *Home Improvement*, then a regular Top 10 series.

Drew learned his first lessons about the downside of prime time—your time slot and your lead-in are two factors that all the talent and all the good writing in the world might not be able to overcome. In the same way that a half hour of a baby's sleeping aired between *Seinfeld* and *ER* would probably rank in the Top 10, being buried on Tuesday against a powerhouse ABC comedy lineup with a lead-in like, oh, say, *Saved by the Bell,* doesn't bode well for the chances of a new show.

"When I heard we had to follow a show like *Saved by the Bell,* that was like having to go to prom with your ugly cousin, you know?" Drew admitted. "You just have nothing to say. 'Drew hated *Saved by the Bell*. And *The Mommies,* too.' You can put that down. I don't care who the hell knows it."

Much to the dismay of producers Martin and Curran, Drew had made a career out of speaking out on what he felt were the world's absurdities and idiocies. In the Book of Drew, *The Mommies* fell into both categories.

The Mommies television show was based on the Mommies comedy duo—Caryl Kristensen and Marilyn Kentz, a couple of suburban housewives turned stand-up comedians. Against all odds and logic, their stand-up routine, which basically consisted of kvetching about upper-middle-class life in suburbia, became popular enough for NBC to develop a show around them after a breakout performance at the 1992 Montreal Comedy Festival.

Ken Tucker of *Entertainment Weekly* deemed the series "the definitive prime-time argument for state-sponsored orphanages."

The Mommies debuted in September of 1993 and despite

scathing critical response, NBC, aware that the two women had a devoted legion of female viewers, picked up the series for the second half of the '93–'94 season. When *The Mommies* was brought up at *The Good Life* press conference, Drew couldn't contain himself.

"*The Mommies* is among the worst, the most pandering, insulting shows to women I've ever seen on television," he ranted.

But gee, Drew, how do you really feel?

"If somebody said to me that this is what we found to represent your group and that's the best they could do, I'd be so pissed. I was very polite about this until they were renewed for a whole season. That's when I thought, *Well, that's it!*

"I mean, here we are a mid-season replacement show and they're going to be on the whole year. That also means they're getting as much money as I am," he joked.

But Carey's tirade was genuine, and he didn't care if he was ranting against his own network.

"I apologize to the executives, but it just seems so unfair to me," he continued. "I know so many, so *many*, female comics that are so funny and really deserve a break and have really been working hard and really working on their craft.

"But the network goes and gets these two housewives out of nowhere and gives them this thing and I don't think they deserve it. I think there are other people more deserving that could have done the same format.

"If they wanted to make a show about two mothers, they could have grabbed two really funny stand-ups—given it to people who really deserve it—and made the same show."

Realizing that Drew had committed the sin of being openly critical of a fellow network show, producer Martin and star Caponera tried to take some of the sting out of Carey's remarks. Speaking your mind, after all, isn't the best way to make friends and influence network executives.

"Why don't we do wrestling on pay-per-view between you against *The Mommies*," Martin suggested.

"So, does that mean you give the show an A *minus*?" asked Caponera.

Carey apologized, but wasn't humbled or bowed. When asked, he gave his honest assessment of *Home Improvement,* too.

"I've seen it, and it was pretty funny. I liked it. But you know, it's like here and there. Sometimes it's just really funny because it's so goofy. And sometimes it's like *bleh,* you know? It can get too sappy. But I'll also tell you, Tim is one of the nicest guys in the world. *He* deserves his success."

Drew was equally forthcoming about the state of television in general.

"I never really watched sitcoms, to tell you the truth. But I forced myself to watch sitcoms when we got *The Good Life* just to see what the other ones were like. And I tell you, I think they suck. I gotta tell you the truth. I really think that a lot of them are horrid and I can't stand to watch them. There."

Carey had thrown down the gauntlet. He wasn't going to be bowed by unspoken network political correctness. If TV wanted him, it would have to take him on his own terms.

Ironically, had *The Good Life* been half as creative and amusing and controversial and biting and perceptive as Drew was at the show's press conference, it would still be on the air. But unfortunately, the individual ingredients didn't cook up into a palatable mix, and it suffered a drubbing both in ratings and at the hands of some critics.

TV Guide was lukewarm:

"Some of their jokes have a tinge of sophistication, a taint of hipness: The boring guys in the warehouse admire PBS's *The Civil War*—which is just the writers' way of saying that this incredibly overrated show was, in fact, dull. In those moments, *The Good Life* wants to be *The Simpsons*: relevant and irreverent.

"But then it turns into *Cosby*, with Dad lecturing his son on life: 'You gotta take pride in what you do.'

"The show tries to be hip . . . but lovable . . . but sexy. The one thing it doesn't try to be is like TV's best sitcoms: real. For these aren't real people getting laughs out of real life. They're caricatures."

Entertainment Weekly was more brutal:

"In a situation comedy built around the styles of not one but two stand-up comedians, *The Good Life*'s Caponera is a better actor than many other stand-ups turned sitcom stars, but he hasn't been given any amusing lines. . . .

"Carey fares worse. Without the material that gives his nightclub act some punch, he spends most of his time standing around grinning sourly. . . .

"It's too bad, because with his beefy frame, buzz cut and square-guy horn-rimmed glasses, Carey is a cartoon waiting to be funny. . . .

"At one point Caponera says, 'There's too many good things in the world.' *The Good Life* ain't one of 'em."

The series was yanked off the air after a few weeks.

"It was really painful for John," says a friend. "Even though in some ways Drew took part of the show away from him, it was John's show. When it failed, the stigma and blame fell on his shoulders. Drew was the guy who walked away with the praise of being the show's saving grace.

"For John, it was probably the end of the road, as far as getting his own series. For Drew, it ended up being one big audition tape."

Despite the less than stellar reviews and low ratings, Carey remains loyal to the work they did on the show.

"I think it was a great show," he says. "Other people thought it was a great show. But we had a terrible time slot, and that's what killed us."

Looking back at *The Good Life* episodes today, it's interesting to note Drew's character: a quick-witted, occasionally smart-mouthed white-collar worker who's a little antagonistic toward upper management. Sound familiar? Drew's *The Good Life* character would turn out to be the rough draft for the character he'd later play in *The Drew Carey Show*.

SEVEN

Drew's goal was still to be a great stand-up comedian. But now he was convinced the best way to do that was to take a prime-time detour.

"I will do anything it takes to be a great stand-up, even if it means doing a series," he had said while doing interviews for *The Good Life*. The failure of that series only cemented his philosophy.

"A television series is all just advertisement for my stand-up career," he explains. "That's why I never changed my name. I don't want someone saying, *Hey, Joe!* when I'm walking down the street because then I'd have to pop 'im." He smiles. "I'd get really mad."

It's actually not that novel an approach. Any comic worth his gags knows that networks have an insatiable appetite for stand-up-turned-sitcom stars. But Carey thinks there's a danger in basing your stand-up act on the hope you'll get a series.

"Gee, yeah, a lot of men and women do, but they shouldn't. Take my act—there are a few things in there we can use on the show, but I have such a nightclub-type act that is freewheeling and filled with dirty language, there's not that much that we could use on the show.

"I've got some great jokes I use in my act that I could never use on television. For example: There is this mountain lion fucking a zebra. And they're up on a big hill and he's going at it with the zebra. And the lion sees his wife coming up the hill from behind and he goes to the zebra, *Quick, act like I'm killing you.*

"Or there's one where two old folks are sitting in the home and the old man says to the old woman, *I bet you can't guess how old I am.* And she says, *Unzip your pants.* So the old guy unzips his fly, the old woman puts her hand in his pants and feels around in there for a few minutes, then says, *You're eighty-three.* The old guy looks at her. *That's amazing. How'd you know that?* The old woman shrugged. *You told me yesterday.*

"If you try to tailor your act as a sitcom audition, the act will suffer. If they're honest with themselves, if they're smart stand-up comics, they'll do whatever they want to do in stand-up to make it honest and worry about the sitcom stuff later.

"Because, if you tailor an act for a sitcom, what you get is *The Mommies.* Seriously. The one thing about *The Mommies* is that they were good marketing people—but that's all they were. And if that's all you have, you got nothing."

It had been over a year since *The Good Life* had folded its tent, and in looking back Drew admitted the experience had been emotionally draining.

"When I did the pilot, I thought, *Okay, I'll do this to get the pilot money.* I never had any idea we'd be picked up for a series. So I was just happy to be on a show and happy to be able to make a mark for myself. *I* was getting good reviews, so I didn't really care," he says, laughing sheepishly.

"This is the weird thing: When you're doing a sitcom, you're so insulated from the outside world and everybody working on the show wants it to succeed so much, it's almost like being in a little cult. All the executives and the director and the network people would say, *Wow, this is great! This is going to be so funny. This is going to be a big hit.* Blah, blah, blah. *Start buying your mansion now.*

"And I really believed everything they were saying. I was like Born Again Sitcom Guy," he says in a deep, superhero voice.

With so many people assuring the cast that they were the next coming of *Seinfeld*, hope and expectations were running high. Then came the show's first air date.

"I remember picking up the paper the day the ratings came out to see how we'd done," Carey recalls. "When I saw the first ratings, I thought, *Oh, my God . . . my life is over.*"

The Good Life had been buried. After the initial shock dissipated, Carey and the other cast members held out the hope that the show would still find an audience. After all, everyone had told them how good it was. They kept their fingers crossed that the network's publicity machine would kick in and help them out.

"We were supposed to have promos for the show air after the Super Bowl that year, in 1994," Carey says. "So we had this big Super Bowl party and everyone is going, *Is our promo coming up now?*

"Nope. We kept on waiting, but they still didn't promo it. And then when it finally came on, we were so pissed. The lowest[-rated] show ever after the Super Bowl. I was like, *Oh, God. . . .* It was miserable."

After *The Good Life* was canceled, Drew didn't sit around moping about what might have been. He went into his version of therapy—club work.

"I love doing stand-up and I hope to do it the rest of my life," Drew says.

Some of the biggest comics-turned-TV stars still regularly retreat to their stand-up roots, some to try out new material, some to keep sharp, some just because they enjoy it.

"Drew is one of those guys who just loves doing stand-up," says a fellow comic. "He's like Seinfeld, whose life is about doing stand-up. To keep his material fresh, he'd come in the Improv with maybe six new jokes on a piece

of paper, get up in front of the crowd and try them out on the
audience. Then he'd do a couple of his old jokes and get off.
He wouldn't stay on stage long, but it was enough to stay
fresh."

"Jerry is a monologist at heart, and he regrets that his TV
show has gotten away from his act. Initially, Seinfeld was
supposed to be half his stand-up act and half his home life.
He had no idea the home life side would completely take
over the show."

As it turns out, Seinfeld has another motive to keep his
stand-up skills sharp.

"He makes a huge, huge amount of money doing corporate appearances. All the big comics do. Say some company
is having a business seminar or convention. They'll hire
someone like Seinfeld to perform as an incentive for people
to attend. He'll get up and do twenty-five minutes and walk
away a hundred thousand dollars richer. Not that he needs
the money . . ."

For Drew, going back to his stand-up was also a way to
gather himself for his next plan.

"I was really happy to get back on the road after the
series, but I was also still plotting to get back on prime time,
too."

But *The Good Life* was not an experience he cared to
repeat. So this time around, Drew would take the lessons
learned from the failure of that show and use them to pilot
a series of his own. The first thing he had learned from his
last experience was that he didn't like being a second
banana; he felt confident enough to take on the responsi-
bilities of being a series lead.

"That was my secret egomaniac inside me saying, *You
have to be the star of your show, like every other comic. And
if you don't, you're just not as good as everybody else.* So
that was my big goal."

And there were plenty of studio and television executives
more than willing to take a chance on Drew. They considered him a solid investment. Not only did he have a
distinctive look but, more important, he really was funny.
And Drew wasn't just funny onstage—he was funny in

general conversation, without having to resort to bits from his act. If half of his humor translated to the screen, the execs knew, they'd have a hit on their hands.

Initially, Disney was the winner in the Carey sweepstakes. The studio teamed him up with "hot" producer Michael Jacobs for a project called *Akron Man*. It was not a marriage made in heaven. Drew desperately wanted his own series on the air, but he knew that he'd probably only have one chance. If he let himself be packaged in a show that didn't let his humor shine through, he figured, his television career would come to an abrupt end. He had to balance his anxiousness to get on the air with the ability to be patient and wait for just the right situation. *Akron Man* was not it.

But the experience was not a total loss. It taught Drew the fundamental importance of finding a producer you trusted and who in turn "got" your comedy. The problem Carey had with Michael Jacobs was that they had two different opinions of what was funny—not a good omen for a proposed comedy series.

"A lot of sitcoms are liked forced marriages," Carey explains. "You've got to deal with the studio and how they work. First, they go, *Oh, you're really funny. We want to be in the Joe Blow business.*

"So they hire Joe Blow. And then they look around for one of these five-million-dollar-a-year producers they have hanging around and they go, *Oh, he's a nice guy. Let's have this guy work with Joe Blow.*

"And they kind of force you together. And then, like a lot of shotgun marriages, sometimes you don't get along so it doesn't work out. You end up getting a big, bitter divorce. That was the experience I had with Disney when I first made my deal with them. But that's how it works with everybody.

"Sometimes it really does work out, but a lot of times it doesn't. The thing is, this is your one big chance and if somebody's messing up the persona you've spent years creating, the character you created on stage, it's like they are messing with you personally. You don't take it as an actor doing a role; you take it as a personal thing. And that's why the talent rebels so much."

Having seen his first creative marriage end in divorce, Carey decided to turn the tables on the television hierarchy. Instead of just being the talent, Carey decided to become a producer and do the show he wanted. Suddenly he became an aggressive partner-searching suitor.

"What I did that was different," Drew explains, "is that I courted people rather than waiting for the studio to play matchmaker. I had an idea of what I wanted in my producer 'mate.' I knew what kind of show I wanted and the kind of working relationship I wanted with a producer.

"I met with a bunch of different executive producers. We had lunch and stuff, but I kept going until I found somebody I really, like, fell in love with and wanted to work with."

The lucky, blushing producer bride was Bruce Helford. It helped that they had a shared past: Helford and Carey knew each other from *The Good Life,* where Helford had worked as a writer. A small, wiry man, Helford first came to Hollywood with hopes of being an actor, after deciding that following in the family business was not for him.

"My parents have been in the pet business for fifty years," Helford says. "But my dad also had a roving pet show called Bird-O-Rama. We'd travel around the country in this big old station wagon with about a thousand parakeets."

There was only one problem with his acting aspirations— he had no acting talent. So he turned to stand-up.

"That was even more embarrassing," he says with a laugh.

So he set his sights on writing.

"In the beginning, that wasn't much better, either. Once I tried to get a job at a place that produces horoscope booklets and they sent me a letter back saying I had no discernible writing ability."

Helford decided to stick it out anyway and started writing spec scripts, which means he'd write an unsolicited screenplay for a television show and submit it. He got his first break when he sold a script to *Family Ties.* His next bump up the ladder came in 1992, when he was hired as executive producer for *Roseanne*.

"I ran *Roseanne* for a year before we had the inevitable Roseanne-producer falling-out," Helford says. "But I learned a lot from that experience and most of the time that I was there was great.

"The biggest thing while I was there, though, was I saw how a producer can get off on the wrong foot with the star of a show. In all honesty, Rosie felt locked out of the process in the beginning with her producer, Matt Williams, and that was a big lesson for me.

"When I met with Drew, I told him that if we did this, we were doing it together, from day one."

That was fine with Drew, because he was looking for more than a business partner; he was also looking for a comedy soul mate. One of the reasons often cited for *Seinfeld*'s success is that the comedian had producer Larry David around to make sure the show's comedy stayed on Jerry's track. They had been partners since before the series aired, and David knew exactly what was right for Jerry and never let the series stray too far from that.

"Yeah, we wanted to copy that total involvement," Carey says. "And that's exactly what we talked about from the first day we talked. I said straight out that I wanted the same kind of working relationship Seinfeld has, where he has a say-so in everything.

"I didn't want a situation where a producer says, *Well, I've done TV for a long time so just listen to me, little guy, and don't worry about it.* I couldn't put up with that at all."

In other words, Drew didn't want a "boss." He didn't want interference from other people, didn't want them telling him how to run his show. Not to worry. Helford is more from the Mickey Rooney *Hey, gang, let's put on a show* school than from that of Otto *You vill do vat I say* Preminger. In all of the television shows he'd worked on up to this one, Helford had gained a reputation for being very nurturing of talent. Which is why he was chosen to work with young stars in two of his series: *Phenom,* about a teenage tennis sensation, and *Someone Like Me,* starring

Gaby Hoffmann. He's known for treating his actors with respect and building friendships that last after the show goes off the air. This was Drew's kind of guy. In Helford, Carey sensed he had found someone he could work with in a long-term situation

"Yeah, I don't like being told what to do," Carey readily admits. "But I like working with people in partnership, getting their ideas and working as a team to hash things out."

"Drew is one of the most genuine and generous guys," says Helford in return. "He's not a screamer or tantrum thrower. Whenever there's a problem, we sit and work it out."

"My relationship with Bruce has worked out great, man," Carey says seriously. "I couldn't be happier. I told Bruce that I was going to be the only comic who has their own show who's going to be fighting to keep his producer *on* the show."

Carey was making a not-so-veiled reference to Bruce's experience with Roseanne, who is notorious for having a revolving door for producers—although in recent years she has lost her diva crown to another edgy stand-up, Brett Butler.

"I am flat-out the main creative source for that show and for everything in it," Brett has said of *Grace Under Fire*. Many times. "So, the network needs to be sweet to me."

It's that attitude that has given Butler the reputation for being, as they say, difficult.

"Brett Butler is by far the worst when it comes to *do it my way or else,*" says one comedy writer. "I know people who have worked for both Brett and Roseanne and the comment you always hear is they'd rather spend a year with Roseanne than a week with Brett Butler.

"With Roseanne, you had to deal with a Dr. Jekyll and Mr. Hyde–type situation. When Dr. Jekyll shows up, everything is fine with Roseanne. But with Brett, every day is a Mr. Hyde day."

Don't think Brett isn't aware of her reputation. In fact, she wears it like a badge of honor. Before *Grace Under Fire* aired, Brett was tossing around some promo ideas for the show.

"I thought it should be, *Hi, I'm Brett Butler—the new bitch at ABC*. They wouldn't go for it."

Helford, though, understands the frustrations that can lead sitcom stars to become difficult and start pulling temper tantrums.

"Drew and I started from a really good place, and that's where the problem has happened with stand-ups. I think there are a lot of producers who are too ego-involved to let a good comic mind get into their process. I don't know if they are insecure or what

"But there is no better way to go than the way Drew and I did, which is to get together in the beginning."

The first order of business for the new team of Carey and Helford was to develop the show's concept, one that Drew could step into without breaking a sweat. Rather than try for a high concept (space alien family comes to suburbia), they kept it simple.

Drew wanted a situation that the audience could relate to and that he was familiar with. He liked the idea of having the character working in a mid-level position, as he had done in *The Good Life*.

"We thought that this is the life that Drew himself would have lived had he not become a stand-up comic," explains Helford.

"If I had never become a stand-up comic, what would my life end up like? I tell you what—I would have some crummy job. One of those jobs that people get where you just show up. It's your first job out of college or high school and you're just there. You punch in every day and get little promotions here and there. You only see as far as you can see—and that's not very far. And that's how this character goes through his life."

With that in mind, they gave the character a job position with just enough authority to make him realize just how not powerful he was, relocated him to Cleveland and made his cohorts singles instead of putting on the air a standard married guy with three kids. It was important to Drew that his character not be angst-filled. He wanted to show that you don't have to have an upwardly mobile career or be a CEO to be happy.

"We were hopeful that people would relate to the show precisely because it's about a guy who just has a job, not a career, but who's still happy and content," says Helford. "We wanted Drew's character to be a real optimist. He's up about his life and moving forward—but moving forward at the pace most people realistically move forward."

Once they were happy with their concept for the show, it was time to try and sell it.

"Actually, it was a lot easier to sell it than I thought it was going to be," Carey admits. "After we sat down and thought out the pitch, we arranged a meeting with Warner Bros. They thought it was a great idea. Great, we have a studio who's willing to make the series.

"Then we set up meetings with ABC, Fox and CBS, in that order, for Thursday, Friday and Monday. After we pitched ABC the idea, we mentioned that we were setting the series in Cleveland. And the network executive thought that was great. He was like, *Finally, a show that's not set in New York or L.A. Finally, there's something different so we can get away from these cities.*

"Having the show set in Cleveland was really an asset. ABC loved having the show set in a Midwest city other than Chicago. Everybody, when they want to do a show about the Midwest, picks Chicago. I don't know why . . . maybe because they're assholes," he reasons, laughing.

ABC executives were so keen on Carey's idea that they begged him to cancel his meetings with the other networks.

"They bought it right away. Now, we had a network to air our series. It was a lot easier than I thought it would be."

ABC put Drew's show on the fast track, with a bullet. Competition among the networks for half-hour comedies is fierce. ABC felt rightfully smug that it had signed one of the funniest stand-ups around, and treated him accordingly. At the time, ABC was not yet owned by Disney, a company notorious for "hands on" supervision of (or as some prefer to put it, interference with) the creative process. Carey was pleasantly surprised that ABC was supportive without trying to take over.

"I've got to tell you, it's such a night-and-day difference compared to places I've been," Drew said before his show premiered. "I always feel that here are people who are really nurturing and they want to help me. And their notes about the show come across that way. I feel like I have people I'm in partnership with, as opposed to somebody who's just ordering me to do something this way or hit the highway."

However, Drew does admit that it was gently suggested that perhaps he should tone down his shoot-from-the-hip, take-no-prisoners opinions about other shows. NBC executives were still miffed over his filleting of *The Mommies* during *The Good Life* press conference.

"Oh, man, everybody told me I needed to be nicer," he admits, with a not-so-apologetic grin. "But I'm telling you, the shows that I thought were bad excuses for a TV show, they were either canceled or who knows what happened to them. Like *The Mommies*."

When it came to *The Mommies,* he just couldn't help himself. To his mind it was the perfect example of all that was wrong with network television. While promoting *The Drew Carey Show*, he joked around with reporters, once again taking aim at the two former housewives from Petaluma, California.

"Hey, what happened to *The Mommies*? I've been looking for them," he said, laughing.

What kept Drew going on about the pair is that they refused to die a quick broadcast death. After their series finally went off the air in June 1995, Caryl and Marilyn got a new deal at ABC, who hired them to host a daytime chat show.

"I don't know how they got back on the air. I wish somebody would write an exposé on *that*.

"You know, there's nobody else that pisses me off as much as them. Even the shows that I wouldn't watch because they're more family-oriented are still basically good shows. They might not be for me, but kids like it. And

I can give it up that way without having to put the show down.

"Like, for example, *Full House*. When that was on the air I wouldn't watch it because it was *such* a family show. But I still thought it was good for what it did. My nieces loved *Full House*. They thought it was the greatest show.

"But nobody liked *The Mommies*," he said, unconcerned that he might be stepping on toes, again. "It was *such* a miserable thing."

So what television shows get the Carey stamp of approval?

"Personally, I watch a lot of news and a lot of sports. My favorite cable channels are CNN, Headline News and the Playboy Channel. I don't schedule my life around the Playboy Channel, but I do like to see what's on.

"And I watch shows like *NYPD Blue* and *Homicide*—it's one of my favorites—*The Simpsons* and *The X-Files*. I hate to tell Warner Bros. this, but I haven't seen an *ER* I really like."

Drew hesitated only for a second or two before deciding, *What the hell.*

"I remember watching an episode of *ER* where the woman has the cesarean section after they can't deliver the baby the other way. We were watching the show and a friend of mine had the best joke—when they were carrying the newborn baby away to the table, my friend goes, *Hot baby, coming through, watch out*. It was like the funniest fucking thing."

It's classic Drew: poking fun at cultural icons, especially ones that take themselves too seriously. Even if they are produced by his studio. But that had been the basis for Drew's comedy career from the beginning. In his act, Drew continued to take jabs at whatever he considered to be self-righteous.

"So, did you have a good Earth Day this year? I had a great Earth Day. I drove around with my muffler off, flicking butts out the window . . . then I hit a deer."

Nothing is sacred. Not Stephen King:

"You get to the end of his book and go, *Pfft, why did I bother.*"

Not all-powerful *TV Guide* and its surreal fan polls:

"Do you *really* think Matthew Perry's eyebrows are two of the greatest things about television?"

The club audiences loved him. Now all he had to do was win over 20 million or so television viewers.

EIGHT

Now that Carey and Helford had been given a go-ahead on their series, Drew became a diligent student of Sitcom 101. He told Bruce he wanted to learn the process from the bottom up in order to be more than a figurehead producer; he wanted to have a hand in every aspect of the series. Helford knew that the backbone of any series starts with the quality of the writing, and wanted Drew to start there.

"So the first thing I did was have Drew come on as a writer for a show I was doing at NBC called *Someone Like Me*," Helford says. "The best way for him to learn the process was to see it in action. It really came in handy later on when it came time for Drew and I to write the show together. He now knows the work that goes into preparing a weekly script. And believe me, nothing is better than when I'm on a stage and Drew turns to one of the actors and says, *Hey! Say it the way it was written.*"

A comedy club acquaintance of Carey says Drew didn't need tutoring when it came to thinking that his way was the right way.

"Remember, Drew's basic philosophy is that pretty much everyone else is full of shit. And that's his attitude toward his writers and even other actors on his show. Let's say John Doe is doing a scene. If he tries something on his own initiative that Drew hasn't suggested or approved, Drew will say, *Oh, yeah, yeah, do it that way, pal. Don't do it my way. I guess the show's going to be called* The John Doe Show *now, huh?*"

Speaking of show titles, one of the most important decisions for Bruce and Drew would be finding the right title for their show. Naming a series can be an excruciating process, as networks, producers and stars try to find something snappy and memorable.

"Quick and catchy always helps," says Warren Littlefield, president of NBC Entertainment, citing examples like *X-Files, ER* and *3rd Rock From the Sun* as titles that wrap themselves around the public psyche and match the tone and tenor of their series.

Bill Coveny, a television programmer, points out that the title's importance goes beyond a mere guide listing:

"You have to think not only about what goes on the air, but about ads, T-shirts, hats and other marketing tools."

Imagine if *Seinfeld* had kept its original title, *The Seinfeld Chronicles*. Or if *Oil* hadn't at the last minute been dubbed *Dynasty*. Fox executives were worried that using an address, *Beverly Hills, 90210,* would alienate economically challenged viewers.

One of NBC's top-rated shows almost missed out on its now-famous moniker. The network was only able to call its show *Friends* after ABC changed the name of *These Friends of Mine* to *Ellen,* which in itself was a noteworthy break in Mouse tradition: Disney historically does not name shows after stars, preferring not to give actors that much visible power.

Consider what happened with Valerie Harper's NBC series, *Valerie*. The show obviously meant to trade on Harper's long-standing popularity. But from the beginning she butted heads with the network and studio over creative matters. As tensions increased, producers renamed the show *Valerie's Family* as a pointed reminder that they who giveth can taketh away. When the situation collapsed completely,

Harper left, Sandy Duncan arrived and NBC changed the title yet again, this time to *The Hogan Family*. The title changes were the equivalent of airing dirty network laundry. And no doubt managed to confuse some viewers.

Despite the concerns networks harbor about naming shows after performers, it's become a common practice, especially with stand-ups going into sitcoms.

"The advantage to self-billing is that it distinguishes the show from all generic titles," says CBS's Les Moonves. "The disadvantage is that people might wonder, *Why are they naming a show after someone I haven't heard of?*"

The "identifiability" factor is exactly why Drew wanted the show to be his namesake.

"I wanted to call it *The Drew Carey Show* and Bruce goes, 'Uh, that's great. That's who you are, that's who the show's about, the one guy, Drew Carey.'

"At first I thought, *Wow, it would be a great idea to have a show named after me,* you know? Then I thought, *Wow, think of the women I'd be able to meet if I had a show named after me.*

"Besides, why can just Seinfeld have a show named after him? I've got an ego as big as anyone else's.

"And then I go around to the set and I see the sawhorses when they're building the set have 'Drew Carey' written on them. You go to the office and it says *The Drew Carey Show* everywhere. And I'm like, *Holy cow. No pressure.*

"That's when you feel the weight of it all. I wish I would have known what this would feel like or I would have probably called it *Cleveland Guy* or some stupid name like that. But the thing is, I really didn't feel like changing my name. Who am I going to fool, you know? I'm not fooling nobody."

Actually, if Drew could have gotten away with it, he wanted to call the series *The Drew F. Carey Show*.

"Yeah, between Bruce and me it was *The Drew Fucking Carey Show*. We were going to call it *The Drew F. Carey Show* and see if anybody would ever figure it out at home."

The setup for the show was this: Carey is the assistant director of personnel at a Cleveland department store, making $26,000 a year. He's worked at the store for seven years and seems to have reached his glass ceiling. When the workday ends, he goes home or to the local bar, called the Warsaw, to hang out with his three best friends—Oswald, Lewis and Kate.

"My character is one of these guys who just wants to do his job and go home and have fun. He's not a loser, but he's not all that successful."

A few weeks before *The Drew Carey Show* premiered, Carey—with Helford at his side—once again sat down with reporters to talk about his new series. He was upbeat and confident and clearly in charge. For the most part, the network had given him almost everything he had asked for—except for its time slot.

Considering his feelings about "family shows," the show Drew envisioned would have ideally aired at 9:00 or 9:30 because of the adult content he wanted it to have.

"We figured all along that it was an adult show, you know, about my life. So we pitched it as a nine o'clock show, where we figured we could get away with a little more edgy language.

"But once we were told it was airing at eight-thirty, we absolutely had to tone it down. On the other hand, nobody's going to stand around and go, *Oh, poop!* you know?" Carey promised.

"Basically, we're not going to be gratuitous with it," Helford added. "If it's really wonderful for a joke, and it feels appropriate, and it feels right for the characters, we will use certain words. But we're going to watch it so the show's not full of gratuitous 'hells' and 'damns.'

"You get, like, a quota. *You can have two 'craps' but we'll give you only one 'damn. . . . Well, if you throw in a 'hell,' okay.* It's that kind of thing."

"Of course with me," Drew chimed in, "it's like, *If you take the 'fuck' out* . . . that's one reason why I prefer stand-up. TV is edited for language and content, so it's harder to be funny. But the bottom line, as far as I'm concerned, is if you don't like it, don't watch it. I say, let them be offended. I just want the show to be funny."

Being funny was the one thing Drew didn't have to work
at. It came to him naturally and, unlike some comics who
say they tend not to be funny except when they're working,
Carey says he's not the kind to mope and be bleak until he
gets onstage.

"You know, being funny is a permanent state of mind,
with gusts up to a zone," he explains. "It's true, you have to
be in the mood to be funny. But most guys I know are
always in the mood—most funny guys, at least.

"We have the best writers in Hollywood. We really lucked
out with them. Plus, we're doing a point of view that isn't
represented much on TV, and that helps a lot. Everybody on
TV seems to have a very cool job, you know? That's not
how it really is."

A year earlier, in 1994, NBC had premiered *Friends*. The
sitcom struck a chord and became television's newest
phenomenon, catapulting its six actors into the pop culture
icons of the moment. The series also became a success
standard against which other shows were compared.

If it's true that imitation is the sincerest form of flattery,
then television producers are the world's biggest ass kissers.
It is no secret that a successful series will result in numerous
copycat shows, some successful, some not. *The Cosby Show*
begat *Family Ties, Full House* and many of the subsequent
"family couch shows." *All in the Family* paved the way for
Sanford and Son, Maude and *Chico and the Man*. *Friends*
was the demon seed for *The Single Guy, Caroline in the City*
and other such series.

This was the prevailing network atmosphere when Carey
and Helford were preparing to launch *The Drew Carey
Show*. Even though Carey's sitcom would turn out to be
distinctly different from *Friends,* in the months before
Drew's show premiered, he had to battle the perception that
his show was just another low-rent *Friends* clone.

"What happened" explains a network publicist, "is that
Friends became a big hit the season before *The Drew Carey
Show* went on the air. They were developed, though, almost
simultaneously. There was all this buzz about *Friends* and
the networks saw that if you show people in their late

twenties and early thirties together—not as couples but as friends and hanger-outers—you can get an audience."

Warren Littlefield, feeling frisky over the *Friends* juggernaut, accused several new 1995–96 shows of being *Friends* rip-offs or wanna-be clones. Among those he singled out was *The Drew Carey Show.* When asked if his show was going to be as warm and cuddly as *Friends,* Drew sighed.

"Well, let's see. *Friends* is a show about young, good-looking people in their twenties and I'm an overweight guy in my thirties. And I'm not that good-looking. But I appreciate the comparison," he said brightly.

"I wish I was in my twenties and good-looking, but I'm not. Our show is about one single guy who lives in Cleveland, who has a gray-collar suit job—which is a blue-collar job masquerading as white collar because he doesn't make that much money."

Helford said he thought the audience would be the ultimate judge.

"Drew's persona, both in real life and on the series, is that of the little guy who goes out to do battle with the big guys and always returns with a shred of dignity. He's a happy sack, not a sad sack. The show's unique."

"Yeah, plus we'll be the drinkingest show on television," Drew added. "You know, I remember when the big complaint was that every family on television had three kids. It was like, *Oh, another family with three kids. Oh fuck, I hate this show.*

"You know, so even though there's me and I have two male friends and a female friend, there are differences. I'm going to have things those other shows don't have, like all at once: neighbors and people and a boss I interact with at work and friends at a bar.

"So I don't know how he gets a *Friends* clone out of that, but if that's what he wants to think . . ."

Helford agreed. "There's no overlap with those other shows, except that he does have friends in the show."

"Yeah, okay. Well, if it will help Warren Littlefield, we can call them 'acquaintances' instead," Drew said, exasperated. "And as far as other stand-up shows, it's too easy to make generalizations.

"The only thing I have in common with Ellen's show is that I'm single. And the only thing I have in common with Brett Butler is that I'm bitter," he laughs. "I could match her bitterness for bitterness, if I ever got the chance."

"I do think the one thing we do have in common with those two shows is that they are pretty much reality-based shows," Helford pointed out. "They're about real people. Ellen's a real person. Grace is obviously a real person— almost to a supernatural degree."

"I've got to tell you, though," Drew concluded. "I don't think our show is anything like *Friends* or *Seinfeld* or any of these other shows."

Certainly, no producer from those other sitcoms ever had to go to Cleveland in the dead of winter for research. But Drew felt it was important for Bruce to get a feel for his hometown in order to give the series just the right tone and sensibility.

"We actually drove to Cleveland together, because I don't fly," says Helford. "The good part was that we found out we could hang out together and be really comfortable."

And the bad part?

"It was in January," says Carey brightly. "At first, ABC and Warner Bros. didn't want to pay for the trip. And Bruce is going, *What do you think? I want to drive to Cleveland in January for fucking fun? You think this is my vacation?*"

And what exactly did they research?

"Basically"—Helford laughs—"Drew took me to a bar."

"Hey, it was legitimate research," Drew maintains with a straight face. "We were looking for a bar to use as a model for our set interiors. So, he needed to see what bars are like in the Midwest."

While, uh, researching, Drew and Bruce stopped in at a local pub called the House of Swing.

"Where swing is king, Lakewood, Ohio," Carey says proudly. "And there was a band of gentlemen in their fifties or sixties who like to play jazz every few nights at a club. They were probably retired from whatever their other jobs had been. One of the guys had written a song called 'Moon Over Parma,' which is about a local neighborhood in Cleveland."

Helford explains for the uninformed. "Parma is the place people in Cleveland make fun of. I was laughing so hard I almost fell off my chair. So we called these guys and we said, *Hi. We're from Hollywood and we want to use your song.*"

"And the guy is like, *Yeah, sure,*" Drew says. "Then when he realized we were serious, he goes, *Ooh, Lord. Hey, Joe.*"

The songwriter, Bob "Mad Dog" McGuire, wrote "Moon Over Parma" as a folksy tribute to the Cleveland area. McGuire, who was given his nickname by a former band-leader after he started howling during a solo, had written the song in the early 1980s.

"I always thought of 'Moon Over Parma' as a bit of local humor—a Cleveland thing, that's it," says Mad Dog. "But they're not going to do it just to sell a few hundred copies in Cleveland. So they must know something that I don't."

McGuire wrote the song, which is about a guy who gives his girlfriend a radish bouquet, for a comedy show on a local television station. It was intended to be a poke at local suburbia.

The song's appeal to Carey meant a windfall for Mad Dog McGuire, who gets $750 to $1,000 every time it opens the show.

"It'll do," he smiles. " I can take a day off with that. It's kind of like having another job but not having to go to work."

Definitely Drew's kind of guy.

Drew took his new partner on a tour of Cleveland, showing Bruce his old schools, his favorite haunts like Bob Evans' Restaurant (which makes one of Drew's favorite meals—beef tips and noodles) and, of course, his old neighborhood and his prized possession, the Carey family home.

"I'm renting it to a friend of mine from grade school," Carey explains. "After I began making decent money in

1989, I had the house rewired. Having a properly working furnace was like a miracle. But now I want to give it a complete makeover.

"I'm putting in a pool, a Jacuzzi, a white picket fence, a fireplace—all this stuff to really deck it out. I'll have the basement redone so I can go stay there and my buddy can still live there. I want to go back to the neighborhood instead of staying in a hotel.

"I'm telling you, if I didn't have the money I wouldn't be doing all this stuff to the house. But I have the money and it's something I always wanted to do.

"I suppose when I'm done, the house may not fit into the neighborhood as easily. When I go back there now, it can't be exactly as it was anyway, because of the TV show. But I'm still going to live there when I'm in town and I'm still going to go to the same grocery store and I'm still going to eat at the same restaurants that I've been going to since I was a kid. You try to hold on to whatever you can."

Not only was Drew acting in the capacity of producer, he also helped write some of the show's episodes, including the pilot.

"We've got a full staff of writers who will be writing episodes and Bruce and I will be writing episodes together, too. I'll go to the writers' room every night to see what's going on and to meet with Bruce and discuss the scripts and rehearsal and stuff. If the show runs a long time, I hope to be writing scripts on my own."

Even if Drew wasn't so anxious to be involved in the show's writing, Helford would have insisted.

"First of all, it's great having him there, because it's important for the writers to learn what he likes, what he doesn't like, what he feels he can do best and not do best. It's to the show's advantage to have that interaction. Which is why I never understood why on so many shows, it's usually, *The star is coming. Quick, pretend like we're doing something else.* That's one of the big differences with the way we run our show."

• • •

As September 1995 and the new season premieres neared, Drew was hopeful that they had put together a show people would like and find funny.

He was particularly happy with the cast of "acquaintances" they had assembled: Diedrich Bader, Ryan Stiles and Christa Miller.

"Yeah, man, they're all great," he enthused. "Diedrich Bader, of course, was Jethro in *The Beverly Hillbillies* movie. *Whoo-oo.* And believe me, he's thrilled every time I bring it up.

"And then Ryan Stiles was on a Comedy Central show called *Whose Line Is It Anyway?* which is such a great show. He's really, really hilarious."

Carey and Helford consider Christa Miller their "find."

"She had only done a little bit of stuff here and there, but I was shocked when she read," said Helford. "She just blew us away. She had been doing modeling but hadn't really launched seriously into an acting career. She's the kind of woman who really does hang out with the guys. She's very athletic and in college played soccer, basketball—everything."

Drew says he thought she was perfect for the part because, "She's just the kind of girl I'd like to hang out with if I was in real life."

Speaking of hanging out with girls, Drew admitted before the show aired that his status as soon-to-be sitcom star hadn't done much for his love life.

"Yeah, nothing. Nobody knows me, because the show's not on the air yet. It's like telling someone what you're planning to do. So when I'm on the air hopefully women will flock to me and go, *Oh, I saw you on television. Tee-hee.* But so far, nothing; women haven't started mobbing me yet. But if you know any mobs of women, please send them my way."

His social calendar aside, Drew awaited the new season with high expectations.

"Literally everything I wanted to have in a show is in the show, except for a couple of minor things that aren't even worth mentioning," he said at the time. "Well, I wanted to be a woman originally, but that's the only thing. Maybe the second season.

"The only other problem we're going to have is Major League Baseball is charging us something like five hundred dollars a pop every time we show something from the Indians. So, that probably won't be in there as much as I'd like it to be. And they want to see the script and all this other horseshit, so you probably won't be seeing much of the Indians in our show."

But other than that, Drew had put together the show he wanted. He knew he had been given the best shot possible. The network and studio had left him alone and given him nearly complete creative control. ABC had given him a choice time slot, between *Ellen* and *Grace Under Fire*. This time, there would be no opportunity for finger-pointing, and Carey knew it.

"If the show flops," he said, "I will take the blame."

NINE

Sometimes, the success or failure of a show can depend on the supporting players. While Mary Tyler Moore was the linchpin of her series, it was her interaction with Valerie Harper, Ed Asner, Ted Knight and Betty White that provided the biggest laughs.

The same is true with Jerry Seinfeld and his costars. Julia Louis-Dreyfus, Jason Alexander and Michael Richards all share the spotlight with Seinfeld and without any one of them, the dynamics and unique chemistry of the show would collapse.

"Seinfeld should get a lot of credit," says a comedy writer. "He hired three of the funniest, most talented people in the business—and let them shine. He was secure enough and a smart enough businessman to do so. He doesn't get credit for that but he gets all the money, so that's enough.

"Jerry has made himself the straight man, just like Mary Tyler Moore. Ted Danson did the same thing—and they all borrow from classic Jack Benny. Make the central character the straight man and let the other people be the funny ones. Rhoda and Sue Ann got more laughs and zippy one-liners than Mary Richards ever did. Jack Benny made himself the butt of some jokes but for the most part, he was the straight man for everyone else.

"But with Drew, he was the one shooting off the one-liners," notes the writer of the show's early episodes. "He was doing Bob Hope. In Bob Hope movies, Bob Hope was the only funny person. Kind of like the way Brett Butler runs her show, too."

But Drew isn't Brett. He wants his costars to get their fair share of laughs. It is true that in the first episodes of *The Drew Carey Show,* he did take center stage, and that should have been expected. Any show has to grow into a rhythm and until it does, the spotlight tends to shine brightest on the central character. Both Carey and Helford believed their supporting cast would mature into solid foils for Drew to play against.

Not everyone shared their view. After watching the pilot episode, one television critic snidely noted:

"They wanted that show to be a mutant combination of *Friends* and *Seinfeld.* So there's a girl with three guys who all hang out together. Christa Miller is Elaine, but without the same level of comedic ability."

Ouch.

Interestingly, almost overlooked in the pilot was Kathy Kinney, who played the then-minor character of Mimi Bobeck, who is introduced when she applies for a position as a cosmetics counter salesperson. When, for obvious reasons, Drew doesn't hire her, Mimi threatens to sue the store. So Drew's boss, Mr. Bell, hires her as his personal assistant.

In the first half of the show's first year, Mimi was mostly a third-tier regular, (think Newman of *Seinfeld*) sharing office scene time with Nora, played by Jane Morris. If there was going to be a "breakout" second banana à la Rhoda or the Fonz, it was assumed it would be one of the Stiles-Miller-Bader trio.

Of the three, Christa Miller got the most initial attention because she was the lone lady among three guys. She also was the least experienced of the three, actingwise.

Miller, the daughter of top 1960s model Bonnie Trom-

Drew and Kathy Kinney take their schtick to the 18th annual Cable Ace Awards in November 1996. Photo by Janet Gough. Reprinted by permission of Celebrity Photo Agency.

Drew shows off his warmer and fuzzier side with some four-legged friends at a celebrity benefit for the Amanda Foundation, a group that saves hard-to-place animals from the Humane Society's "death row" and finds them homes. *Photo by Gilbert Flores. Reprinted by permission of Celebrity Photo Agency.*

Drew chats with reporters and shows off a tasteful paisley tie at a December 1996 comedy benefit at L.A.'s famed Improvisation comedy club. *Photo by Roger Karnbad. Reprinted by permission of Celebrity Photo Agency.*

Drew flashes some skin with frequent date
cosmetologist Elena Mazzachella while
attending the 23rd People's Choice Awards
in January 1997. *Photo by John Paschal.
Reprinted by permission of Celebrity Photo
Agency.*

Drew and Jeff Foxworthy share the 1996 People's Choice Award for favorite new sitcom star. *Photo by Kevin Winter. Reprinted by permission of Celebrity Photo Agency.*

Drew and Kathy Kinney *sans* Mimi makeup at the Take a Chance with Stars event in November 1996. *Photo by John Paschal. Reprinted by permission of Celebrity Photo Agency*

Drew leaves the suit and tie at home and goes casual chic for a night on the town. *Photo by Ed Geller. Reprinted by permission of Celebrity Photo Agency.*

Drew joins the A-list crowd at the November 1995 premiere of *Casino* in Los Angeles. *Photo by Miranda Shen. Reprinted by permission of Celebrity Photo Agency.*

Drew and date Renee Raudman arrive at the 1996
People's Choice Awards. *Photo by Janet Gough.*
Reprinted by permission of Celebrity Photo Agency.

Mr. Promo takes a moment to plug his show while attending the January 1997 Golden Globe Awards. *Photo by Lisa O'Connor. Reprinted by permission of Celebrity Photo Agency.*

peter, was raised in New York City by her mom, her parents having divorced when she was two. At ten, she survived a rare benign bone tumor that required surgery and radiation treatments.

Miller actually began her modeling career at six months old when she did a Wonder bread ad with her mom. At four, she appeared on the cover of *Redbook* and in a famous Ivory soap advertisement shot by Francesco Scavullo. But it wasn't as if she and her mom were a team.

"My mom told me I was very bratty," Miller says with a laugh. "So it was rare when we did jobs together. My mom never wanted me to model at all. She really didn't want me involved in show business at all."

"I know she has a lot of resilience—she proved that with her illness," explains Trompeter. "But as far as a career in show business, I wasn't so convinced that she would continue to have the necessary determination in the face of the odds against it happening.

"I knew the kind of rejection involved and I knew it might never happen for her. I didn't want her to be miserable—I wanted her to be happy."

After the Ivory soap pinnacle, Christa took a break until she was a high school teenager before working again, this time at the suggestion of top modeling agent Eileen Ford, who happened to be a family friend. She got her first commercial, for Polaroid, when she was sixteen.

But Trompeter was not amused that her daughter was spending so much time in front of a camera. After a JCPenney ad campaign (with Phoebe Cates) during summer break, Bonnie pulled the plug.

"When I went back to school, my mom called up Eileen Ford and said, 'Chris does not do this anymore.' I was so angry; we had a huge fight."

Fortunately, Miller had an outlet for her frustrations—even when she was working as a model, she had been an avid athlete, playing basketball, softball, volleyball and tennis.

But after graduating from high school, she was free to decide for herself, and started modeling again. In addition to doing magazine work in America, she also worked regularly in Europe and Japan. But it wasn't an exciting, jet-setting kind of lifestyle. Miller says the modeling world is not the free ride many assume it is.

"You have to be really into it and disciplined. I was neither. The truth is, I've always wanted to be an actress, but I got a late start."

So while still doing some modeling to pay the bills, Miller turned her real attention to acting.

"I did a lot of *really* bad plays," she says of her first efforts. "I forced people to come watch me in *really* bad plays. Actually, one person came, got dragged by a friend of mine. She was an agent and hated the play, but liked me. So I went with her agency."

In a way, Christa was following in one of the family businesses. Miller's aunt on her dad's side is Susan Saint James, who at the time was starring in her own television show, *Kate & Allie*. According to both Miller and Saint James, Christa auditioned for a role on the series without Saint James's knowledge. (Be-lieve it or not!) Miller got the part, playing, according to Christa, "a nightmare, the preppy girl from hell, for two episodes. She moves into Kate and Allie's house to sublet their apartment in the last season."

"That was done completely on her own; I didn't even know about it," Saint James swears. "TV is about having personality, and Christa's got a good one."

But the former *McMillan and Wife* star also admits that she's given Miller some words of advice that echo Trompeter's concerns.

"Christa gets mad at me sometimes because I tell her determination and survival instinct, the ability to hang in there, are as important as talent. But I think it's true. And I also think Christa has that in spades."

In 1991, Miller moved to Los Angeles to try and make a career happen. She appeared in guest spots on a number of shows, including *Northern Exposure, Fresh Prince of Bel-Air* and *Seinfeld,* as well as some B-movies like *Kiss & Tell* and *Stepfather 3*.

"In *Fresh Prince* I played a girl who was hanging out

where Will's character was working at the campus store. It was a small part. But at the end I had to dance with him, which was very embarrassing for me because I can't dance.

"And when I did *Seinfeld,* that was really scary. You know, the sets are much smaller on the stage than they look on television. And I was sitting there thinking, *I'm really in Jerry's apartment.* I was really intimidated and shy."

She has told friends that the audition for Drew's show couldn't have come at a better time, because she was down to the last of her savings.

"Kate was one of the first roles I read during pilot season that was really great. As soon as I read it, I worked on it and knew it was something I wanted to do," Miller recalls. "So I faxed the script to my friend Matthew Perry—from *Friends,* ironically—and he helped me out."

Perry shrugs off any credit. "Christa's cute, funny and quirky, and that is a rare and wonderful combination. I knew she was eventually going to get on a show. I think I gave her one piece of advice, which she either followed or she didn't."

Christa begs to differ. "He helped me decide Kate had to have a really hot temper. She doesn't take crap from anyone. That was really key, as it turned out."

"It was a normal audition like any other one I had, but then I kept going back and back—I went on five grueling auditions before I got the part. But I really did nail it.

"Now I get to go to work every day and I belong somewhere. I have a group of people I love, who I get to see every day. When I'm feeling the most tired is when I'm the most grateful."

Ironically, Christa says, now her mom is making up for lost time as a stage mother.

"I was back in New York visiting and while I was there, I was scheduled to do Conan O'Brien's show. The day before the show, I was talking on the phone to some friends and every five minutes my mom is going, *I think time would be better spent thinking about your Conan interview than gabbing on the phone.*

"And that was the whole vacation. I was like, *When did this start? Now you're Brooke Shields's mother?*"

Viewers will have noticed that Carey's series alter ego is obviously sweet on Kate. And since Drew by his own admission is not really an actor, does this mean that Drew himself is sort of sweet on Christa? When asked, Miller takes the fifth.

"No comment." Then she adds, "Drew and I are very good friends."

During an interview, Carey let slip some of his affection for Miller when they were asked about their on-screen relationship.

MILLER:
I think Drew and Kate are best friends and have been best friends for a long time. I think Drew would probably go for it, given the opportunity, right?

CAREY:
Yeah, I think so.

MILLER:
If I wasn't very drunk.

CAREY:
(with a shy laugh) I think in real life and onstage.

As for her thoughts on Carey, Miller is warm . . .

"Drew is very, very, very funny and he's as nice as he is funny."

. . . but careful. When asked if she has feelings for him beyond friendship, she keeps it simple.

"No." Then she adds, "There is a boy I have a soft spot in my heart for, but I don't know what's going on. I'm very busy at work and it's very distracting. I hardly have time to go hiking with my dogs, so I certainly don't have much of a social life. My regular schedule is to get up at eight, read the script every morning because they put in changes, and then rehearse all day, go home and if I'm not too tired, go to dinner. Pretty boring."

Drew seems to be content to have an unrequited crush on Miller because of how much he enjoys her as a person.

"She really is someone I would hang out with. And when Dick Ebersol's your uncle," Drew adds, referring to Saint James's husband, who heads NBC Sports, "you know a lot about sports, man. Whether you like it or not. She loves watching sports and stuff, which I think is great.

"Christa's kind of like me. We're both really comfortable sitting at home reading. I like that. And she doesn't look really glamorous."

And she can be as clueless as any of his guy buddies.

"One day she was complaining about some foul odor in her trailer," recalls Carey. "Ryan Stiles asked if she checked the fridge. She had and there was nothing there. Then he asked if she had checked the microwave.

"She got this blank look on her face. There was roast beef that had been in there for over a week."

Drew isn't the only guy who appreciates Miller's brand of sexy.

"The audience response is crazy, especially if there are men there," Christa says. "At first it was really overwhelming and it still makes me laugh. It is quite flattering, but I personally don't get it. When guys say, *You're so sexy on that show,* I'm surprised, because I'm wearing jeans and flannel shirts all the time.

"Maybe men relate to someone who's not so perfect or dressed up. Maybe that is sexy—a girl who's one of the guys.

"Christa does have a tomboy quality to her, the way she moves and stuff," agrees Drew. "She's played a lot of sports in her life. What you see is what you get with her, although in real life she's more 'girlie' than what you see on the show."

When he was born, Diedrich Bader's dad might have envisioned his son following in his footsteps as a career politico. William Bader was chief of staff for the Senate

Foreign Relations Committee and is currently president of the Eurasia Foundation on Capitol Hill. But when he was four years old, Diedrich gave the first indication that he was more his mother's son (she's a noted sculptor and artist whose work is featured in Washington's National Gallery).

When he was two years old, Bader's family moved to Paris because of a political appointment his father received. In France, the toddler was taken to movie theaters that played classic American films, including silents by Charlie Chaplin and others. One night, as Bader family lore tells it, a reel of film from a Chaplin movie burned up in the theater's projector, rendering the screen black. During the technical intermission, the four-year-old climbed up on the stage and amused the crowd with an imitation of the Little Tramp. He received a standing ovation and according to Diedrich, his fate was sealed.

Bader stayed in France until his early teens, when he came back to America to attend high school at the North Carolina School of the Arts. While hanging out in New Mexico during spring break, Diedrich was approached by a casting agent, who arranged for him to audition for a small role in a pilot that was filming. Diedrich didn't get the part—he got a starring role instead.

The pilot wasn't picked up, but Diedrich was hooked. He moved to Los Angeles and found work guest-starring on television series, including *Fresh Prince of Bel-Air, Cheers, Quantum Leap* and *Star Trek: The Next Generation*.

"I was on the episode called 'The Emissary' that introduced Worf's lover when he became captain of the ship," Bader recalls. "I took over his position. I never got to walk through the door, but I did get attacked by Klingons."

A turning point in his career came when he was hired for director Penelope Spheeris's series *Danger Theater,* a spoof of action-adventure films. Spheeris remembered Bader's comedy talents from when she was casting *The Beverly Hillbillies* feature film. In it, Diedrich played dual roles as Clampett twins Jethro and Jethrene.

Unlike *The Brady Bunch* film, which became a camp hit, *The Beverly Hillbillies* was a misguided effort that is best forgotten, as far as Bader is concerned. When asked by a fan during an on-line chat whether he was worried *The Drew Carey Show* would typecast him as a wacky best friend, Bader, who plays Oswald, a deliveryman-wanna-be-mobile-DJ, was unconcerned. "Better that than Jethro," he said.

Bruce Helford reveals that Diedrich is so anxious to put *The Beverly Hillbillies* way far behind him, he asked if he could please not wear plaid shirts on the sitcom. "He says he wants to shed the image."

Besides being grateful for the chance to make amends for Jethro, Diedrich is simply happy to finally be on a series.

"This was my seventh pilot," he says. "After a while, you begin to wonder if it'll ever really happen. When it does, it's the best, really."

Seattle-born, Vancouver-raised Ryan Stiles shares Carey's stand-up background, which he says gives them a similar outlook.

"It's the same kind of work ethic. Drew and I both have the attitude that if the audience believes we're having fun, they'll have fun. If it looks like a pain in the ass having to be there, they're not going to have fun."

Despite being a good student, Stiles became restless his senior year of high school and dropped out a few months short of graduation, then quickly got a job doing stand-up. Unfortunately, he never made a name for himself as a club comic, because his timing was off.

"My first [gig] was at a stand-up club in Vancouver in 1976 and I stole all of George Carlin's material. I did it for a lot of years and was actually able to support myself. But I was doing stand-up when it wasn't really popular. Right after I decided to get out, it really went through the roof. Not a good career choice."

From stand-up, Stiles segued into a different kind of comedy performance. In 1986, he became a member of the Second City comedy troupe in Toronto, which featured future *Saturday Night Live* and *Wayne's World*'s star Mike Myers.

In 1990, he moved to L.A. to perform with the Second

City group based there, working alongside Jim Belushi, Robin Williams and Robert Kind of *Spin City*. It didn't take long for Ryan to start piling up film and television parts, including a recurring role on *Mad About You*. He's also the host of the comedy/improvisation show *Whose Line Is It Anyway?* on Comedy Central.

With his improvisation background, Stiles, who plays Lewis, a maintenance man for a large pharmaceutical company, has often been asked if he finds it hard to stick to the script.

"When we first put an episode on its feet, we improvise around the script, but by show time, it's pretty well set." Then he adds, "Unless it's a week where I don't have many lines—then everything caves in."

In a serious moment, he credits Drew with being the main reason the show has taken off.

"I think the thing that makes the show work is that Drew's really not a threat to anybody. To women, he's kind of like a big teddy bear, to men he's kind of like a sportsy, jocky guy, and to older people he's kind of like their son working to make ends meet."

Although Stiles has worked a lot in both film and television, he says he's happy to have a steady gig for now—especially since he, wife Pat and their two kids have a four-acre ranch in a small farming town in Washington and he is only in L.A. when he works.

"This gig will allow him to be able to live where he wants without worrying about being able to afford it," says a pal.

After so many years of working in relative obscurity, at least on a national level, Stiles appreciates, perhaps more than his costars, the opportunity to have a regular television gig.

"I like both television and film, but if I had to choose, I would pick a sitcom every time. They both have their good points, but TV is quicker and you don't have to wait months to see your work." Stiles pauses, then adds, "But out of all the visual mediums, I prefer working with a sketch artist."

The Drew Carey Show debuted quietly. Saying that it was not an immediate success is a polite way of saying the show hit the ground stumbling. *Variety* saw potential but was critical of the supporting players.

"Kate (Christa Miller) is the snappy-looking tomboy whose blatant talk isn't as smart as writers Carey and Helford think it is.

"The kitchen's the meeting place to talk over activities, but the talk's routine, the reactions predictable.

"Carey's affable and some of the stuff is funny. But a car-pool seg doesn't work and the talks around the kitchen are ho-hum, at least in the opener.

"Future depends on stronger verbal sallies among the principals and on giving them something to do other than parley."

People magazine voiced similar reservations about Carey's costars.

"Drew Carey is funny—even before he opens his mouth. With his four-sack body, bad military-academy haircut and severe, black-rimmed glasses, he looks like some gravy-stained driving instructor from the 1950s. . . .

"The show's weakness is a negligible supporting cast, particularly Diedrich Bader and Ryan Stiles, who are all too repulsive as the slobby friends with whom Carey likes to throw back a few brewskis after work. The producers are clearly trying to remedy this problem. Since the pilot, they've dragged in a pack of brain-damaged yahoos as neighbors. That hasn't helped, but I hope the salvage work continues, because Drew Carey *is* funny."

Critic David Vermillion echoed the sidekick theme.

"Carey's stand-up roots serve him well in scenes where he's making wry observations. But in scenes where he has to interact with other characters, his acting is awkward and unpolished.

"Carey's not accustomed to sharing the stage with other performers and the script adds insult to injury by ignoring the supporting cast. It leaves the three friends with nothing to do but nod their heads at Carey and laugh. Only occasionally do the writers let them chime in with jokes of their own.

"Of Drew's friends, Bader shows the most promise and

Stiles suits his character well. Miller, however, is not very convincing as Kate. Her acting is choppy and her delivery is off at times. But surrounded by such talent, she will probably fine-tune her character soon.

"The show's greatest strength is Drew Carey himself. Even though it will take him some time to adjust to his new medium . . . While his trademark short-cropped hair and thick-rimmed glasses do not immediately mark him as a television star, he certainly has the potential to change this perception."

Despite the problems with the supporting players, the general consensus was that Drew was a funny guy and the show had potential.

"If you don't know anybody as hip, cool, and sexy as the beautiful people on NBC's hit *Friends* (and who does?), then comedian Drew Carey's new sitcom is for you.

"Set in unhip Cleveland, this half-hour comedy centers around four lifelong buddies who sweat through life's everyday hassles while sharing a two-story home in the suburbs.

"Drew is your average Joe, with an expanding gut, dorky glasses, and a geeky crew cut. His job, too, is average— assistant personnel director for a department store. But in spite of his bum boss and annoying carpool mates, Drew tries to make the best of things.

"While Drew and his pals are likable, there's something missing here. Originality, for starters. The one-liners and tirades delivered by Carey sound more like monologue material than dialogue—which is exactly what you'd expect when you take a stand-up comedian's act and try to stretch it into sitcom situations and conversations. Everything seems a bit forced."

A comedy writer says the criticism directed at the early episodes was justified.

"The best sitcoms in television history—Roseanne, Mary Tyler Moore, Seinfeld—all have had strong costars and allowed them ample opportunity to shine. Just look at the number of Emmys won by Laurie Metcalf, Betty White and Julia Louis-Dreyfus.

"But Ryan, Deidrich and Christa . . . aren't getting to do anything to speak of."

Without strong costars to feed off of, the show would continue to lack zip and sustained spark. Where would Archie Bunker have been without Meathead? Or Hawkeye Pierce without Hot Lips?

There were other inherent problems to be overcome as well. The most obvious is that stand-ups are used to working alone on stage; for them, learning to share the spotlight with other performers is always a challenge.

Another challenge is speaking dialogue written by others. Drew was used to working from his own material. And even though he helped write a couple of the early scripts and sat in on the story meetings, it was still an adjustment.

"I like to think I can do both," Carey says.

Helford is diplomatic. "Look at it objectively. Drew's grown a lot as an actor as we've gone along. In the beginning, he would say to me, *I can't say that. I wouldn't say that.* And now, it's like, *Oh, yeah, I can find a way to say that.*"

"It's all a different discipline. There's no way to compare the two," says Drew. "Both are rewarding and I like doing both, for different reasons. I still like doing my stand-up the best because even though that's scripted, I can still veer off anytime I want and talk about whatever I want in the middle of anything. Like now.

"O. J. is trying on the gloves, right? And they don't quite fit, because they shrunk and he can't get them on his fingers. And he goes back to the defense table and looks at Shapiro and says, *Gee, Bob, maybe I didn't do it.*" Drew laughs at his own joke.

"It's a lot more discipline when you're doing the scripted stuff for TV. When I'm doing the show, I have to stand at a certain place so the camera can pick me up and the light is right and all that stuff, or we have to do it over again."

Which brings up another hurdle for stand-ups going into television: The mere process of filming a sitcom episode can be troublesome for a television newcomer. Even though there is a live studio audience, the actors are really playing and performing for the director. If a scene doesn't work, they do it again. And again. And again—as many times as it takes. Audiences can get worn down and lose their sense of humor as the taping drags on. It's no easier for the performers. Even veteran television performers can lose their comic edge as the night wears on. For sitcom newcomers, it takes time to become "tape-night tough."

For the first half of the 1995–96 season, *The Drew Carey Show* languished in the middle of the Nielsen Ratings pack. It was neither a breakout hit nor an embarrassment. It was just . . . there, with nothing special to set it apart.

The spark that would kick-start the show's writing and viewer interest was just a "Bite me" away.

TEN

As 1996 approached, *The Drew Carey Show* continued to tread ratings water near the middle of the pack. Despite some moments of sheer hilarity, the show was still uneven and lopsided, with Drew carrying most of the comic weight. The most balanced episodes were ones that resorted to what's called stunt casting—bringing in well-known performers to fill guest-star roles.

In one episode, Kate's feud with one of Drew's old high school pals threatens to ruin his birthday party, until she surprises him with a special gift—arranging a visit from his idol, baseball player Dave Winfield.

"Meeting Dave Winfield was such a thrill. I was standing there thinking, *I'm so glad I have a show*. Otherwise I never would have been able to hang out with him.

"That's the only reason I want to have Albert Belle on," Carey continues, referring to another star baseball player. "I just want him on so I can say I met him—and I want to have him autograph a bat and stuff. I swear to God, that's the truth.

"No offense to Dave Winfield, but we actually tried to get Albert Belle first, but he wasn't available."

Throughout the season, familiar faces popped up in surprise roles: Jamie Lee Curtis showed up as Mimi's fashion-challenged hairdresser and Susan Saint James, Christa's aunt, guest-starred as Kate's mother. In the fifth episode, Drew got himself in legal hot water after he taped up a cartoon that a female colleague found offensive and she charged him with sexual harassment. The following week found Drew being urged to settle by the company's attorneys, played by Penn & Teller, who provided some much-needed comic support for the star. Later in the season, Tim Allen made an appearance—the only guest spot he's ever done.

"You have to be really careful about how you use people," Drew admits. "But we didn't really care how implausible it was that Tim Allen would actually land in my tree, because it was Tim Allen. The crowd went crazy. We thought it would get a lot of people to watch the show.

"Let's face it, that was really blatant stunt casting. I mean, we talked about him falling in a tree and were like, *So what, if we get Tim Allen on the show!*"

Helford acknowledges that stunt casting can sometimes be perceived as a sign of weakness in a series that doesn't have enough of its own backbone.

"I know it's a questionable thing because it really isn't your show and those people aren't going to be there week to week. But when you get to play with those people, it's really fun. If you're going to have those characters in the show anyway, why not get the most wonderful people available to play them?

"We're getting calls. People want to come play on our show now."

Unfortunately, not enough people wanted to come *watch* the show. Even so, despite the unevenness of the series, it was still slowly winning converts. *TV Guide* critic Jeff Jarvis offered this mea culpa.

"When the show started, I thought we were in for a male Roseanne, an Archie Bunker, Jr.—another highly paid actor trying to act blue collar, trying to fake being real. But I misjudged Drew and his surroundings. As it turns out, the show is more like TV's version of 'Dilbert,' the hot comic strip of the 90s. Both are sly, truth-filled comments on life at work in the age of downsizing. . . .

"He is a book that should not be judged by his cover. . . . What separates this from the more serious, sermonizing sitcoms of the era is that Carey doesn't use his show to whine about his life or change the world."

In fact, changing the world was the last thing on Carey's mind.

"I do not have a social agenda for this show," he says. "I mean, we'll have shows about stuff that really happens, like the sexual harassment episodes, where you put up a cartoon or some wrong kind of thing at work and you inadvertently offend someone. And then all of a sudden, this little incident turns into a big brouhaha. But I wasn't making a statement about sexual harassment; we just did that as a story device, that's all."

Helford says his aim is to take the little, everyday irritants that everyone goes through and use them to get some laughs.

"The stories we do actually happen to people, and that's what we try to tap into: office problems, strikes, trouble with your plumbing—just anything people really go through, to make the humor more relatable."

It's not surprising that Carey's show was often compared with "Dilbert," Scott Adams's strip about a put-upon office worker that has become this year's phenomenon. Adams himself noticed the resemblance and at one point mentioned in the *Dilbert Newsletter* that he noticed there was a "Dilbert" cartoon on Drew's office wall in one episode and that he was considering putting Carey on the Enemies List.

When Carey heard about Adams's remark, he E-mailed the cartoonist asking that he not be placed on the list, and in exchange offered to place some "Dilbert" mementos on the set of the show. Adams agreed, and in a later episode, "Dilbert" and "Dogbert" dolls are clearly visible. Adams went so far as to name Carey "Saint Drew of Sitcoms."

A vital element of establishing any new show is promotion, both by the network through on-air ads and by the stars

of the show themselves. This was one area Drew enthusiastically joined in. After all, if somebody was throwing a
party, he was more than happy to attend.

One such event was sponsored by *People* and held at the
L.A. Planet Hollywood. For the occasion, Drew agreed to
go on-line and have a chat with fans, live from the event.
Carey is very computer-literate and frequently surfs the
Internet on his Mac. In fact, sharp-eyed viewers might have
noticed that on Drew's TV desk, his computer's make is "M
C Tosh." The producers didn't want to have to pay Macin-
tosh a product-placement fee, so they simply covered up a
couple of letters.

So, when *People* asked, he was more than happy to sit
down at the provided laptop and give his cyber-fans a taste
of Drew:

DREW:
Hey, great party here. I have to leave soon, though—
Bruce Willis is about to sing. Just kidding. The food
here is great—I had a rack of lamb and some Chee-
tos. Yeah, rack of lamb, free beer and some kind of dip
that I'll puke up in the morning.

FAN:
I'm eating Chee-tos, too! I'm also eating bacon.

DREW:
Chee-tos and bacon??? What's the international Internet signal for vomit? :0 . . .

After introducing himself and urging people to watch his
show, Drew announces:

DREW:
FREE FOR ALL @ WILSHIRE AND RODEO DRIVE!!!
People are swarming the barriers!!! No lie!!! They all
want to get to Bruce Willis before he sings . . .

What's he got to sing the blues about? *I got those low down, dirty twenty million a picture blues, I got those, ain't it a shame—Demi wants to do me blues. Oh, woe is me. My limo done broke down blues.* Or maybe it's *My hair done left me blues.* I'm talking trash about people I don't know. What a slime I am. You know, in case Bruce sees this and wants to kick my ass.

Later on, Drew gives the cyber-crowd a rundown on the other celebs in attendance.

DREW:
This is really a cool party. I saw Traci Lords! And Tim Allen says hello. When you consider all the other stuff Traci was doing while she "acted" . . . And I'm telling ya, Roseanne is here with her writers, you know, so she can make conversation . . . Chuck Berry forgot the words to *Johnny B Good* at the Rock Hall Concert . . . oh, Bruce Willis is dancing with Chuck Berry now. He's got so much soul . . . : : : :sigh: : : :

FAN:
Is Chuck dead yet?

DREW:
He probably wishes he was—anything for a tribute issue. Hey, time for a wine cooler.

Refreshed, Drew types on.

DREW:
I haven't seen Sly or Arnold—up close, that is. I'm not famous enough yet. "Sly, baby! Loved you in *Stop or My Mom Will Shoot.* Sly! Oscar man . . . what a hoot!"

When it's suggested that this may be the last Planet Hollywood–hosted party he will ever be invited to, Carey verbally shrugs.

> DREW:
> I'm sure he has a great sense of humor. That's what I hear, anyway. I mean, if he can't take a joke by now . . . jeez. :)

As the series was generating increased notoriety and Drew was developing a reputation for his hilarious observations, and as the show entered into its second half, some much-needed zip was being supplied by a then-minor character named Mimi Bobeck, played by Kathy Kinney. Mimi came into Drew's work life when she applied for a sales job but was ultimately hired as the assistant for Drew's boss, Mr. Bell. Garish, ballsy, with a chip on her shoulder the size of Rhode Island, Mimi would become the bane of Drew's office existence.

At first, their encounters were infrequent, almost afterthoughts. In fact, several reviews of the pilot, such as this one, didn't even bother to mention her name:

"The debut's plot found Drew trying to defend himself against an ugly, pushy woman who was applying for a job in the cosmetics department. Drew knew by her eyeliner that she was woefully unqualified. Although not the most complex or intriguing story line, this did give rise to some rather hilarious moments."

But it didn't take viewers long to take a shine to Mimi. Realizing the one-liner gold mine they had, the staff began writing more with Mimi in mind. In the sixteenth episode, "Drew's New Assistant," they made her Drew's new assistant so the pair could have more acerbic interaction.

"It was always in the plan," claims Helford. (Be-lieve it or not!) "We discussed it when we were writing the pilot, that if the Mimi character worked out, it would make a good regular character to have at work."

"Yeah, we always knew," says Carey. "But it was always

dependent on what actress, so we couldn't really say for sure who the Mimi character was going to be. We didn't know how wonderful Kathy was going to be. In fact, we didn't even know Kathy was going to be Mimi."

Kathy Kinney was actually the third actress to play Mimi.

"It was really funny," recalls Helford. "We had brought in a lot of people to test for the role. Mimi Number One came in and the actress didn't work out when we were on the stage. So I spoke with the director and told him to hire the fifth woman. 'Remember her?' And he goes, 'Yeah.'

"So they brought this actress down and she was the wrong person."

Carey chimes in. "Yeah, we rehearsed it one time with this actress and the director and I are sitting talking on the office set and he goes, real casual, 'Well, you know, there's really something wrong with the way this thing is built. I have to talk to the stage designer and have him fix it to get the right camera angles so why don't we take a little break.'

"And when the woman walked away, the director grabbed me and whispered to me, 'That's the wrong actress!' "

"So she got paid and then fired, right on the spot," says Helford.

Finally, the director brought in Kathy.

Most actors coming into a show late talk about how welcoming everyone is. Kinney admits she had a slightly less warm reception.

"The very first day I came to work, there was another actress on the show, not Christa, who said, 'If you make it through lunch and they allow you back on the lot, you will have really done something.'

"And I just went, 'Oh, thank you,' because I didn't know the history of all the firings. So I thought I could go out to lunch one day and not be let back on the lot."

Not very likely. As the first season wound down, Mimi's exposure was cranked up dramatically. She became Drew's foil and sparring partner. And with each passing week, her makeup became bluer, her clothes louder and her screen time longer.

"She nails every single line," praises Carey. "She never

misses a line. Every line we give her, she makes funny—
even lines that aren't supposed to be funny. She makes it
funny just by her take on it.

"You know, that's the way anybody gets a good role in a
sitcom. Let's say you're on a show and the writers give you
what you think are crappy lines. Don't go, *I can't make
these lines funny.* That's the wrong attitude. The right
attitude is, *How can I make these lines funny and fit in
better?* And that's what she does really great: Everything we
give her to say, she turns into something funny."

"They originally wanted Mimi to be just mean," says
Kinney, "so I based her on the naughty, mean little girls I
had known growing up. After my mother mentioned that
I was one of those mean little girls, I realized she was right:
I definitely alternated between *Look at the pretty kitten* and
poking someone. So ultimately, I made Mimi immature."

Which is a perfect match for Drew, because his humor
can sometimes be that of an angry twelve-year-old. But the
audience loves that and it's part of Drew's appeal. His
relationship with Mimi is just like two kids going at each
other, sticking their tongues out at each other and going,
Nyah, nyah, nah, nyah, nyah.

"The only reason I can make fun of her is that the
audience knows she can take it—and she can give it back.
Mostly, *I'm* on the defensive."

Mimi's favorite comeback, "Bite me!" has become Kinney's signature saying.

"Now people will actually come up to me and ask me to
sign 'Bite me' on their shirts," she says, laughing.

However, Kinney soon discovered that playing an over-
the-top, unique character can cause people to blur the line
between fantasy and reality.

"People always ask me, Are you Mimi now or are you
Kathy?" Kinney says, bemused. "And I tell them, you know,
without the eye shadow I'm just Kathy."

"Just Kathy" says it's a good thing she was born with a
sense of humor. "I come from Wisconsin and I'm allergic to
dairy products. Fortunately, I was raised near a brewery."

Since raising cattle or farming were out as career options,

Kathy indulged herself in her passion for gadgets and working with her hands.

"In high school, I was a techie," she says. "I used to run the follow spot for the town ballet. I also know how to run all kinds of power tools—I put myself through college being a carpenter. I can also rewire things and make lamps and stuff like that. In fact, I have a thing about electricity; I've been shocked so many times, but I love working with it."

She got her first brush with performing at college, when she was coerced into appearing in a production of *The Boyfriend,* playing the middle-aged Lady Brockhurst. The experience was not an epiphany.

"No, I didn't suddenly realize I *had* to act."

She didn't consider a career in entertainment until she moved to New York and a friend talked her into taking an improvisational comedy class. This time, she did have an epiphany.

"It changed my life."

She found out she was funny and could make people laugh. While Kinney did improvisation by night, she continued working a variety of odd jobs to keep a roof over her head and some money in the bank.

"I used to be able to type around eighty-five words per minute," she says proudly. "I did lots of things: I worked as a publicist for WCBS, I was a bartender, worked at a factory, I was a live-in for a crippled ex-*Vogue* model and I was an office worker for the American Psychiatric Association. We got free psychiatric there—which I didn't use, thank you."

After she appeared in the film *Parting Glances* for a director friend of hers from her improvisation class, Kinney moved to Los Angeles in 1987.

"I really stumbled into acting, thanks to the movie. Because it turned into a small hit, it helped my career take off. But when I first came to town in 1987, my agents used to send me out on a lot of retarded-girl stuff. Me and Amanda Plummer, you know?"

Fortunately, Kinney lost out on the demented roles and

had little trouble finding guest-starring work on a number of comedy series, including *Seinfeld, Grace Under Fire* and *The Larry Sanders Show.*

"Even so, I still listed my occupation on my tax returns as a secretary until just a few years ago," she admits. "I think I'm still a little baffled as to why people think I'm funny. I used to be afraid that if I figured it out, I'd lose it. Now I don't worry about it, I just go with it."

Kinney finally felt comfortable enough to quit her day jobs when she was cast on *Newhart* for two seasons.

"I was the slutty town librarian, Miss Goddard. I also tried to blow up Brian Benben on *Dream On.*"

Despite working regularly, Kinney was still just a mostly anonymous character actress until Mimi thrust her into the public consciousness.

"It's shocking to me, and slightly embarrassing, that people recognize me all the time. They used to apologize, *I'm sorry, are you on* The Drew Carey Show? And I would go, *Well, yes I am. How did you recognize me?* It would be my voice, and I'm just surprised."

So as her recognizability increases, Kinney says she's thankful for Mimi's questionable fashion sense.

"I'm glad for all the makeup, because when it's time to put it down, I'll just wash my face and leave Mimi behind."

Of course, washing off Mimi's face takes more than just a splash of water.

"Oh, it used to take forever but now—and yes, this is a plug—I use Chubs, those baby wipes, and I wipe it right off."

Putting on her Mimi face doesn't really take that much longer than most women spend putting on makeup.

"You know, it only takes about twenty minutes to do the makeup and about another twenty to do Mimi's hair, which is very important to her. I think she thinks she has a soft heart, and she's definitely into kittens. And she's a kitten of a gal.

"The thing with Mimi is," Kinney adds about her alter ego, "she's just pretty much a child with a box of crayons."

"A box of crayons with all the paper ripped off," Carey interjects.

"Exactly," Kathy says, laughing. "Chewed off. She would chew that paper off. And you know, I just see her staying that way. She just reacts. Everybody's against her and she's just always fighting for herself, especially against Drew.

"That's just my impression of her. She has a very soft heart . . . it would just take you about fifteen years to get to it."

It seems as if Kathy spends a lot of time explaining and defending Mimi. While most television actors fight against being confused with their characters, Kinney has embraced hers. In fact, Mimi has given more interviews than Kinney. Here's a typical question-and-answer session with Mimi.

Q:
Do you have any beauty tips?

MIMI:
Never stay within the lines.

Q:
How do you pick your jewelry?

MIMI:
If we were meant to wear small jewelry, we'd have been born with tiny rocks in our ears. Jewelry is supposed to be big, to catch the light.

Q:
Where do you get your makeup?

MIMI:
I make it all myself from chemicals I have in the basement.

Q:
Are you a feminist?

MIMI:
Yes, I am a feminist. I would never sleep around unless
I was asked by the right person.

With her larger-than-life character, some wondered if
Carey worried that Kinney would ultimately upstage him.

"No. Because I'm supervising producer and my name's
on the cover of all the scripts," he jokes. "No, she's always
going to be great. And people like Mimi, so the writers have
to come up with a lot of Mimi scenes. That's the straight
answer. It's like Urkel on *Family Matters*.

"However, when I renew my contract, I am going to have
it worked in that I always get a dollar more than her."

Truth to tell, there was some fallout over Kathy's increased visibility, when it was decided that another series
regular, Jane Morris, would not be brought back after the
season ended.

"Originally, it was Jane they had Drew sparring with at
the office," says a friend of Morris's. "She played a
secretary and Drew basically just made jokes about her. It
seemed like he was being mean-spirited because Jane's
character, Nora, was based on weakness. Nora was really a
pathetic person, so it wasn't funny. Sometimes it was
actually uncomfortable, because Nora was so defenseless.

"But the great thing about Mimi is that she has come-
backs. Mimi is like Drew—*I hate the world so fuck you.*
She also thinks everyone else is full of shit. She's got to
come from a position of power, because it's no fun if you
insult someone and they don't fight back."

Kinney speculates on the popularity of her character.

"I think Mimi helps women to find their voice. It's
important that women don't take any crap, you know?"

So Mimi was in, and Morris was out.

"Even though Jane understood their decision creatively,
she was still devastated. She has two kids and she thought
this was her big break. What makes it even more painful is
to watch the show keep going up and up in the ratings.
Instead of being on the gravy train, she got left at the station

with her bags dumped on the platform. It's absolute murder for her.

"But for the producers, they lucked out with Mimi, because Kathy is excellent."

A comedy writer points out that Carey's interaction with Kinney dates back to some classic routines.

"The whole Drew-Mimi thing goes back to vaudeville," says the writer. "W. C. Fields had a bit he used to do with a heavyset woman where insults would fly. She was a big, heavyset woman who was a waitress. Fields would be drinking and eating and every time she'd come over, he'd make some unflattering remark about her appearance and she'd talk about his nose.

"So the Drew-and-Mimi interplay isn't an original concept. It's a great comic promise that was born years ago."

Whatever its pedigree, Kinney is just grateful to have a regular job. She also says she's lucky to be on a series with comics who don't mind sharing the one-liner wealth.

"The thing Bob Newhart knew, and I think Drew realizes it, too, is that the funnier the people are around you, the funnier *you* look and the better the show is. I loved working with Bob. He was just very shy, just like Drew. As Kathy, I would say Drew is also very fun. However, as Mimi, I would say he sucks."

The war of words between Drew and Mimi was the basis for their interplay. But their ever-escalating barbs forced Helford to do some tap-dancing with the Standards and Practices people.

"Doing trade-offs with them goes on with all shows all the time," Bruce sighs. "They ask you, obviously, to stay within certain bounds, especially during certain time periods. Regardless of what you might read in the paper, there's a lot of concern at the networks about what's being said at what time.

"But when you are trying to be competitive with other shows like *Friends,* which airs at eight but still does more adult, edgier material in hopes of attracting adult audiences, you have to be competitive."

Drew says it was never his intention to try to have the

dirtiest show on TV. "But I know for a fact that a lot of times writers will write the scripts with extra language in it, hoping that Standards and Practices will go, *Okay, let's take out these really bad words*. And then the writers get to keep in the words they really wanted in the first place."

"It's very hard to get the word 'bastard' in, or the word 'bitch' in. We've been lucky with the word 'ass,' though," Helford explains. Then after a pause says, "This has to be the most ridiculous conversation I've ever had as an adult.

"But truly, I do find myself on the phone saying, *Well, we'll trade you . . .*"

Drew remembers one bartering session with Standards and Practices.

"Mimi was going to call Drew a butt-wipe. She called me a butt-wipe and the guy said, *You can't use butt-wipe*. He goes, *You know you're wiping somebody's butt*. He made a real strong argument against calling someone a butt-wipe. But he let her call me a butt-weasel. I don't know about you, but to me, 'butt-weasel' sounds worse.

"It's these kinds of conversations that are so surreal. Sometimes Bruce will see me on the stage during a run-through and he goes, *Hey, we got to keep 'ass' on page 42*. He'll be real excited that they let us keep a word. It is a weird conversation."

Despite the absurdity of it all, Helford understands why the networks play word games.

"It has a lot to do with context. What they ask us to do is make sure it's really important to the scene, and I totally agree with that. There is no reason to put foul language on the air for no reason. I don't want my kids saying those things, either."

Interestingly, despite living in the age of political correctness, when any perceived slight of a group can erupt into protest, Carey says the slings he and Kinney hurl at each other hasn't generated any outrage from some offended group.

"No, overweight people don't complain," he says with a shake of the head. "Not that I know of. I actually got a couple of letters on the Internet that say, *It's nice to see someone of normal size on TV.* I never make fun of Mimi's weight unless she does it first. Like I said, *I'm* the one running for cover from *her*."

As May 1996 rolled around, Carey and his crew kept their fingers crossed that ABC would renew their show, even though it finished its first season ranked forty-fourth.

Some predicted the show would go the way of the Cleveland Browns. Paul Schulman, whose Manhattan agency buys TV time for advertisers, already had his eulogy prepared, predicting that Drew's show would be canceled

"I think anyone who's going to get the ax deserves it. Very few shows have terrific writing. Those that do, prosper."

Obviously, Schulman is no seer. Plus, he didn't look at the big picture. What the show had going for it was network confidence in Drew, a breakout character in Mimi and a growing legion of fans—even if those fans hadn't yet translated into ratings. Also in Drew's favor was the general slump being experienced by the four major networks. Over forty new shows had premiered in the 1995–96 season, most of them numbingly similar and indistinguishable from one another—and the next season promised to be a repeat. At least Drew's series had the potential to stand out from the crowded pack. Plus, that March, viewers voting for the People's Choice Awards voted Drew their favorite actor in a new TV series (a title he shared with fellow stand-up Jeff Foxworthy).

In a vote of confidence and with fingers crossed, ABC renewed *The Drew Carey Show* for a full season.

ELEVEN

Relieved that the show had survived an uneven first year, Drew spent the summer hiatus being seen at Hollywood functions and enjoying his newfound celebrity. Even though he'd been a well-known stand-up for years, television had made him a more familiar household face. Fans would shout hellos to him walking down the street and kids would approach him for autographs.

"The thing about Drew," says one autograph hound, "is that he'll actually talk to you. He doesn't just scribble something and walk away; he makes you feel like he appreciates the request."

Drew says he enjoys the interaction.

"I think I'm so lucky, because I've got the greatest fans, man; they are really cool to me," he says. "I used to wonder about it, because you often hear these horror stories from other people about awful people coming up to them. But nothing like that has ever happened to me. I think it has something to do with the vibe I, and the show, put out."

Being a television star was good for some cool perks, too. He suddenly found himself being invited places just because he was Drew Carey. And thanks to the Dave Winfield stunt casting during the first season, some of his longtime sports idols were volunteering to come on the show.

"I went to the Olympics in Atlanta and found out that Charles Barkley wants to be on the show," Carey said during an interview during the summer of 1996, going into his stand-up, storytelling cadence. "I met him when we were both at the House of Blues. He was there, smoking a big cigar, you know, getting in shape for the games, because the Dream Team was giving it their all.

"So, he's like drinking and smoking a big cigar and he's walking around and says, *Hey, when are you going to put me on the show?* And I go, *You want to be on the show?* He goes, *Yeah.* And I go, *Well, you're on, buddy.* So, I already promised him.

"I think if we can get Charles Barkley and Albert Belle, we should have them on the same show and have them come to the hangout and that'll be the episode when Lewis or Oswald will have to get a job waiting tables and they'll start throwing stuff on them, you know, hitting them on the head accidentally and Charles and Albert turn out to be really polite, nice guys.

"Well, it's just a thought."

And in keeping with tradition, Drew was asked if he had a *Mommies* update.

"You mean Caryl and Marilyn, *Real Friends*?" he laughed, referring to their new talk show. "I have to say I saw their new talk show a couple of times and I have to say I think it's their best work."

Drew's summer vacation produced a couple of other highlights. He and Bruce made another cross-country trip to Cleveland, this time renting a Mustang convertible for the drive.

Among his pit stops this trip was his would-have-been alma mater. He visited his old college haunts, at least those he could remember, and stopped by his former frat house. Even though he didn't graduate, Carey had retained ties with his fraternity, but since his television career had taken off, he hadn't been able to visit as much as he'd have liked.

Perhaps that was a good thing—seems like Kent State and Drew were a volatile party mix.

"The last time I went back to Kent State was during the homecoming parade," Carey recalls. "I was drinking in a rented Lexus and I hit someone else's car. It was on a hill and I didn't see him. I knocked out his headlight."

Delta Tau Delta's president at the time, Brad Currence, was thrilled to meet his fraternity's favorite member and gave an effusive interview to Kent State's campus newspaper.

"He was hilarious. He really is a funny guy. You'd just sit there and talk to him and he comes back with all these one-liners."

Whenever he visited, Carey would take the time to help some of his frat brothers who asked for advice. Carl Ferrara, who was a radio/television production major, remembers Drew giving him pointers on how to get started in comedy.

"He gave me advice like wanting me to do amateur nights when I got up to the next level. He said I could call him up anytime for advice. Drew is a genuine guy who never forgot who his friends are."

Ferrara had only met Drew twice when Drew gave him and a friend free tickets to a 1993 New Year's Eve performance he was doing in Los Angeles.

"He's a real good guy and he always remembers where he came from," says Carl. "He's done a lot for Cleveland."

But he isn't generous strictly to frat brothers. According to other comics, Carey is generous with young up-and-coming stand-ups, taking the time to give them an encouraging word about their acts.

"Drew is known for befriending kids who are just starting out. He'll kid around a lot more with the beginning comics than he will with the more established stand-ups. Drew still sets himself apart from those guys."

Maybe because Carey has a soft spot for the struggling and disenfranchised. A source on the show tells the story of the night Drew took the time to lend a sympathetic ear to a fellow Marine.

"One night after a taping, Drew is told that there's this

guy in the audience who's refusing to leave unless he gets to talk to him. You know, at first everyone was kind of nervous because you never know what kind of crackpots are out there."

It's a legitimate concern. Because television stars come into people's homes on a weekly basis, they are probably more likely than others to become the victims of stalkers or mentally ill fans who create fictional personal relationships with them.

Typically, female performers are more susceptible. Sharon Gless was stalked by a woman who eventually barricaded herself in Sharon's home, armed with a gun. Fortunately, Gless was at husband Barney Rosenzweig's house at the time. Theresa Saldana, later of *The Commish* fame, survived a near-fatal attack by a knife-wielding fan who claimed God had told him to kill her. Rebecca Schaeffer, who costarred as Pam Dawber's younger sibling on *My Sister Sam,* was shot and killed by a drifter named Robert Bardo, who had taken an if-I-can't-have-her-nobody-will fantasy to a deadly extreme. Madonna was stalked for years by an obsessed fan who claimed he was her husband. He was arrested and sent to jail after he broke onto her property, toting a gun, and was shot by one of the singer's armed security guards.

While male celebrities aren't usually subject to the same kind of violent stalkings, they can still find themselves the unwilling object of a fan's desire. A particularly sad case involved a mentally ill woman who left her Midwest home and came to L.A., she says, to be with the man she was supposed to marry. She ended up homeless and says she suffered beatings and rapes at the hands of homeless men. And the man she was supposed to marry, who she was still waiting to come get her? Burt Reynolds.

Probably the best-known stalking case against a male television celebrity is David Letterman's experience. For years now, Letterman has been benignly stalked by a woman who keeps breaking into his house. No matter what restrictions or threats the court metes out, she makes her way back to Letterman's house. The talk-show host jokes about it, but it must be unnerving to never know when your home might be invaded by an obviously troubled person.

So when this young man in Drew's studio audience refused to leave, it sent a nervous tingle through many of the production staff. But Drew decided to go see what he wanted, especially when he learned the kid was a former Marine.

"It turns out the guy had just been discharged," recalls the source. "He was depressed and was really having a hard time adjusting to life outside of the service. He didn't know what his future held and felt aimless.

"Drew sat there and talked to the guy for about an hour and a half, listening and giving words of encouragement. He really did understand what the guy was feeling, because he had been there himself. Except Drew hadn't had anyone he felt he could talk to. So he made sure this guy had a friendly shoulder to lean on so he wouldn't do something as stupid as Drew had tried with the pills."

It's not the first time Drew has tried to help others understand their depression. On April 23, 1996, Carey joined William Styron's wife, Rose, and other speakers at the tenth annual Mood Disorders Research and Education Symposium at Johns Hopkins University. In addition to being a medical symposium for doctors, its purpose was to increase public acceptance of depression and other mood-related disorders, and it was open to the public. When asked to attend, Carey accepted without hesitation.

"If he can help one person out there to turn their life around the way he did, Drew will gladly give any amount of his time," says a friend.

As September and the new season premiere date neared, Drew and Bruce prepared for their second year. They hired a few more writers and made a wish list of guest stars they'd like to have on the show. There was a buoyant sense of optimism among the cast, because an interesting thing had happened over the summer of 1996: People had started watching reruns of *The Drew Carey Show*. One critic noted how many people were suddenly writing in about this "new" show they had come across. Going into the 1996–97 season, the series got a boost from the positive word of mouth being generated by freshly converted fans.

One sure gauge of a performer's or television series' place in 1990s pop culture is the Internet. As popularity goes up, so do the number of dedicated web pages and Usenet discussion groups. Although Drew doesn't have the rabid following of, say, Xena, Warrior Princess, he does have his fair share of sites dedicated to him and his show. What's more telling is the type of web pages devoted to the stand-up.

One of the more amusing sites is *PicPal's Drewalike Contest.*

"That Drew Carey . . . why should he get all the good liquor just because he's famous?

"Drew Carey's TV persona is of an easygoing guy on the outside, with a spiteful kid on the inside. We're all like that underneath. But wait, we're not here to heal your inner child. We're here to buy it off.

"It's not a look-alike contest; it's a Drew-alike contest!

"You don't need horn-rims and a buzz cut, or to even be a white guy, or a guy, period. Carey's a state of mind."

(For those curious about the winner, you can check it out at http://picpal.com.)

Not all the sites are so whimsical. The Drew-Mimi combo has brought out the naughty in some Carey fans, including one would-be Henry Miller who scribed an X-rated fantasy involving Drew, Mimi and an erotic encounter.

Apparently, this is a source of curiosity among quite a few fans—namely, what *would* it take for Drew to sleep with Mimi?

Carey shakes his head, as if he's answering a pesky first-grader. "No. It would be a big syndication package—as in a *record-breaking* syndication package."

Then again . . .

"Yeah. Sure, why not? It'll be a *Very Special Drew Carey.* The third season will be all our romance and then we'll break up at the very end of the season, then she'll start dating a psychiatrist. If it'll help the ratings, I'll do anything."

Even dance. Wanting to build on their blossoming following, Carey and Helford had a unique surprise up their sleeves for the second season premiere—the first-ever sitcom musical/dance number. Choreographed to the 1960s hit song "Five O'Clock World" by the Vogues, dancing workers streamed through Drew's office, which turned into a disco, complete with mirror ball and girls in a go-go cage. Carey, displaying some nimble dance moves of his own, sashayed through the two-and-a-half minute extravaganza, obviously enjoying himself. All those nights disco-dancing at college had finally paid off.

The idea for the sequence evolved during Helford and Carey's cross-country getaway to Cleveland.

"We were in the car and the song came on the radio. I don't know, we were just talking about what a great song it was and how it related to our show and we just thought what a great way it would be to open our second season," Carey explains.

"It was really hard to tape that sequence," recalls Christa Miller. "First of all, none of us can dance. The rehearsing was fun, but it was really hard to shoot because it meant all of us had to get it right at the same time. The go-go cage I was in was put up so high I was getting dizzy."

Not all the cast members had to shake their money makers.

"Ryan Stiles has a congenital back problem that can get pretty severe," says a friend. "So on the dance sequences, you won't see him shimmying all over the place. But he tapped his toes to the beat."

The number was such a hit, with viewers and critics alike, that ABC reran the episode a month later and subsequently gave the okay for another (expensive) dance sequence, this time to the Tower of Power song *What's Hip?* at a cost reported to be in six-figure territory. That dance number included cameos by Flip Wilson, Dick Wilson and H. R. Pufenstuff.

• • •

The second season brought better ratings and some story line changes, the biggest being Drew and Kate's breakups with their respective mates. Kate's Jay takes a job in another state; Drew's Lisa moves in with him in an attempt to save the relationship, which turns out to be a disaster, and they mutually decide to split.

Some fans were upset at the departure of Katy Selverstone, who played Lisa. But Drew felt that having his character in a committed relationship took away too much of the comedy potential.

"Yeah, I'll start dating different women and stuff. But it won't be like dating for one show, like other shows do, where you date somebody, find out they have a tic then break up with them at the end of the show. We're more normal."

But don't look for Drew and Kate to turn into the next Ross and Rachel. Despite some indications fans of the show might like to see them together, Carey is quick to point out that he doesn't want their characters' chemistry to change the way it would have to if they had a romance.

"It's like one of those things; we're the kind of friends where we're like *best* friends. If we ever did have sex, it would ruin everything, and we know that so we don't. That's the only thing keeping it from happening—the friendship is too important."

Also written out were Drew's strange next-door neighbors, played by Ian Gomez and Kelly Perine, and Blake Clark, who was Jules.

"He's one of my better friends in stand-up comedy, but I don't think it was working. They were all great, but it was so broad compared to the rest of the show."

Helford gives another reason. "The world was getting too big; it was getting too hard to give everybody enough to do."

Most neglected were two of the main costars, Diedrich Bader and Ryan Stiles.

When asked if their characters would get more of a screen

life in the second season, Stiles said wryly, "I'd just like to find a character first before I try to figure anything else out. I'm hoping that will happen this year. I had a girlfriend for two episodes last year, Pam. What happened to her no one knows. . . ."

Although Stiles might have joked about it publicly, according to a friend he was less than amused about his incidental role.

"Both Ryan and Diedrich hate the fact that every time they get a script they don't seem to show up until page 13. Among themselves they joke that their biggest lines are, *Hey Drew, wanna go to lunch?* Or, *Hey, Drew, what are you doing tonight?*

"The reason they wrote in these characters in the first place was a reaction to the *Friends* phenomenon—you gotta have hangout friends. But the question begs, Why are these guys there? If they disappeared, would anyone notice?"

Carey admitted they were trying to get Ryan and Diedrich more involved.

"It's one of the things we've talked about in meetings with the network, and one of the things they asked about was getting more stuff for Oswald and Lewis, to give them more of a life and flesh out their characters."

In the meantime, Stiles and Bader had become the set's Fric and Frac. Rather than get stressed about being so overlooked, they entertained themselves. During one on-line interview, they waxed poetic about working with Drew:

DIEDRICH:
He's really a woman.

RYAN:
All soft and sweet-smelling.

DIEDRICH:
He loves when you coo in his ear.

RYAN:

He's the type that when you took a bath with him, he'd take the tap in his back.

When asked what the funniest thing that had happened to them on the show was, Stiles said, "A sandbag dropped on an extra once. That was pretty funny. He's a regular on *Homicide* now."

One of their inside jokes is playing with the studio audience about whether or not Lewis and Oswald are closet lovers.

"We'll be this close to kissing," says Stiles. "It's *Are they or aren't they?* We're not, but we do it for the crowd's benefit. It gives us something to do."

One way to get the two guys more involved was through Drew's new beer business. At the end of the first season, Drew attended a small-business fair and on a whim, decided it would be fun to open a microbrewery in his garage. After trying out different ideas, Drew and his buddies decided to brew a coffee-flavored beer: Buzz Beer—Stay Up and Get Drunk All Over Again.

In addition to the housecleaning, there was one major addition to the cast for the second season. In the final episode of the first season, the store Drew works at, Winfered Lauder, is bought by a Dutch company. The only person fired is Mr. Bell, who viewers get to see for the first time is Kevin Pollak, best known for his role in *The Usual Suspects*. Pollak is an old poker-playing buddy of Carey's who agreed to do the voice of Mr. Bell as a hoot.

Ironically, the reason they wrote out Mr. Bell was because everyone thought a pilot Pollak had filmed was going to be picked up. It wasn't. So Craig Ferguson joined the cast as Drew's new boss, Mr. Wick.

"It cost us so much money to actually see Kevin, we got a cheaper, English guy," Drew jokes. "Actually, I don't know why we have a British boss when the Dutch own our company, except we just think British actors are funnier than Dutch actors."

Even though Mr. Wick is the embodiment of all that's wrong with upper management, Carey says he personally doesn't hold any grudges from his days as a working stiff.

"The truth is, ninety percent of all businessmen are really decent people with families, just trying their best. But most of the television audience watching are not people in charge. So you have to give them something and someone to root for. And the way to do that is to make the boss an idiot."

By far the biggest change in the second season was the full emergence of Kathy Kinney's Mimi. More and more of the episodes put her in the center of the action, rather than just reacting to it. Instead of fans' talking about "Drew," it was now "Drew and Mimi." Magazines did dual features about them, ABC promos featured the pair and they even teamed up to do a November sweeps stunt casting of their own on *Lois & Clark: The New Adventures of Superman.* In it, Drew is a con artist real estate agent, with Kinney—as Mimi—along as his cohort.

Kinney was still at a loss to explain her character's appeal.

"There's just something about her people like," she says with a shrug. "I think it's that everyone has anger they want to voice."

Whatever it is, not all viewers—or reviewers—were enamored of the increased emphasis on Kinney's character.

"Drew Carey's comic timing is wonderful, making so-so lines come alive, and the ensemble is uneven but not annoying," wrote one critic. "The danger is the 'Fonz Factor.' Just as the character of the Fonz took over *Happy Days* until it was unwatchable (except by fans of that particular character), Mimi seems to be taking over *The Drew Carey Show.* What made her character work was that she was a constant irritation, a burr under the saddle, but lately the writers seem to think that she's riding the horse. . . . Sure, I like salt on my steak, but that doesn't mean I want a whole spoonful of it."

But according to one show insider, Drew knew better than to tamper with what got them where they were.

"Drew doesn't want to kill the goose that laid the golden egg."

In the autumn of 1996, it seemed like Drew Carey was everywhere. In October, he performed at Walt Disney World's twenty-fifth anniversary party. Refusing to soften his edge just because he now had a hit series, Drew didn't spare the House of the Mouse in his act. Here's his description of how to enjoy a do-it-yourself visit to Disney World without having to leave your home:

Drive the entire family five blocks away from home and park. Walk back home. Then walk around in a circular line for a few hours. Then walk back to the car. On the way, burn your money.

In November Drew hosted the Cable Ace Awards—and turned out to be the life of the party. After the awards, Carey was feeling his oats, telling everyone he was thrilled to have met "my friend Wally"—Walter Cronkite.

Have a few more beers, Drew.

But Carey had reason to celebrate. *The Drew Carey Show* had arrived. In December 1996, ABC Entertainment president Jamie Tarses announced that she was moving the series to the coveted 9:00 time slot on Wednesday. In addition to being a slap on the back, it gave the show slightly more script freedom, because it was now officially in the "adult hour."

"Now we won't have to sit with Standard and Practices trading them two *'asses'* for a *'damn,'*" says Helford. "But other than that, I don't see much of a change. ABC's been great about not restricting us anyway."

Restriction was a hot topic in the summer of 1996. That was the season of the *Public Morals* flap, so there was a lot of discussion going on about what exactly is appropriate language for prime-time television.

The commotion began when a character in the Steven Bochco sitcom uses the phrase "pussy posse." When TV critics saw a preview tape of the episode sent out by the network, you could hear teeth grinding all over the country, although truth be told, the most insulting aspect of the whole thing was how dreadfully, painfully unfunny the episode was as a whole—which made its language seem that much more objectionable.

Unlike Bochco, Drew wasn't interested in trying to push any envelope. He didn't have to—his show rested on its humor.

"We're just trying to be funny, you know? I mean, if they want to substitute dirty words for funny, that's okay. I like dirty words, too—but only if they're funny in the context of everything else.

"Like in my act, I do dirty stuff, but it's always funny. If they're just going to have words to be shocking and not have it funny, nobody's going to watch anyway."

Now, on top of being a comic, Carey proved to be a prophet as well. *Public Morals* disappeared after only an episode or two. But the fuss about language struck Carey as somewhat disingenuous on the network's part.

"You know, you can't say a brand name like 'Coke' or 'Pepsi,' because they're worried about advertising. But, you can say 'pussy.' That's because nobody sells it in a bottle. But believe me, if they sold it in a bottle, you wouldn't be able to show the logo—it might cost 'em money."

Later it would become clear that moving *The Drew Carey Show* was done in part so that *Ellen* could move to 9:30 in preparation for her character's coming out and revealing she was gay. But, DeGeneres's bombshell aside, it was mostly a reward for the show's emergence as a bona fide sophomore hit, indicating the network believed it would be able to provide *Ellen* a strong lead-in.

The Drew Carey Show was now getting nearly universal praise.

"Ferociously funny," screamed the *New York Times*.

"Drew Carey is currently riding high now that his self-titled ABC sitcom, which was on the verge of being canceled last season, is enjoying banner ratings," applauded *Mr. Showbiz*.

One of the more astute critiques was printed in the journal *America*. "The draw is the show's star, Mr. Carey. Like Mr. Seinfeld, he is no Robert De Niro. But neither is he a slouch playing comedy. Best of all, with a frame that the Sears catalog used to call husky, a brush cut and glasses, he looks like an average Joe. He's a nice guy, too. And that, in particular, makes him enough of an alien on television to deserve his success."

Now that his show was a Top 20 program, Carey felt vindicated, although he says he'd expected the series to need some time to grow on viewers.

"I think our show is an acquired taste; it's not your normal show. I think people have to see us and get to know us. And I don't think a lot of people know exactly what the show is about until they watch it.

"But I'd rather it have been like this than have an insta-hit because of our time slot. Like '*Suddenly Susan* I owe it all to my time slot between *Seinfeld* and *ER*.'"

What Drew wasn't thrilled with were the reviews' inevitable comparisons between his show and *Friends*.

"Man, I hated that. I used to rip up magazines and kick walls over it. It got me sick. Because *Friends* isn't all that original; it's a white version of *Living Single*. It is. They didn't invent anything, they just had a good slot, and got popular in part because of that.

"I think critics were lazy and stupid that year. Or maybe they were drunk. There's no way you can think our show is anything like *Friends*. You may as well say *Gilligan's Island* is like *Friends*. And while I'm at it, I have this theory that there's no such thing as 'Must See TV'—on any network."

Now that *The Drew Carey Show* was a proven hit, the other networks got busy trying to come up with Drew clones. In December 1996, it was reported that the Fox network planned to develop a sitcom based on Scott Adams's "Dilbert" comic strip. The release described the show as poking "fun at corporate culture through the bottle-glassed eyes of a lowly engineer."

Hmm, sound familiar?

"Television cannibalizes itself," says Bill Croasdale, president of the broadcast division of Western International Media (in short, he buys TV ads for companies). "You remember the first year after *The Cosby Show*? Every network went out and produced a black sitcom. The idea was *Get me the next* Cosby. Then it was *Get me the next* Friends, *the next* ER. But usually, the newer versions don't work."

Drew was truly in a class unto himself.

TWELVE

The first season the series was on, Drew was so busy trying to get the show on its feet, he didn't really get to play as much as he might have liked. And if there is one thing Drew still likes to do, it's play.

"I'm loving it," he said then. "It's like winning the lottery, but you can't quit your job. Financially, you have more freedom, but at the same time, I'm working ten to twelve hours a day. I don't have time for anything except for promotions. Don't get me wrong, I like doing them because they're good for the show and there's alcohol, but you can't really let loose and get drunk."

But once the series settled into a Top 20 show, the pressure eased and Drew was able to relax a bit and enjoy the rewards of his labors. He finally moved out of his minuscule apartment, the same apartment he had lived in since he and Jackie had broken up, and into a house. For the first time in his adult life he was settled enough to actually entertain the notion of having a pet.

"Yeah, I want a dog and a cat. I think that'd be really cool."

He also looked forward to buying a new car, but not a Bentley or any other status car.

"A lot of people think TV stars drive expensive cars, but celebritywise, most of them go for a fun car rather than an expensive car, like Ford Broncos," Carey explains.

He was ABC's golden boy, star of one of their highest-rated newer series. He had visibility, a good sense of humor, a nicely padded bank account and was suddenly on everyone's A-list.

"Yeah, my life's changed a lot, man. I got more money. I mean, it's been nice. People recognize me and I get good stuff. Christa and I got to go to the Olympics and we got really good seats, just because we're on a TV show."

Drew enjoyed the freebies and being included in Hollywood events, but he still saw the absurdity of getting too wrapped up in it all.

"The coolest thing about being on TV are the perks." "Like, I got to see *Independence Day* at the world premiere. I was in the front row center, so technically, I was the *first* person to see the movie. That's the only good thing I could think of sitting there like this," Carey says dryly, tilting his head back so that it's practically perpendicular to his body.

There was one freebie that Drew ended up paying dearly for.

"You want to hear a funny story? This is true. I went to the Tyson-McNeely fight in 1996 as a guest of Showtime," he said.

"You know, I have the same manager as Tim Allen and he's on Showtime all the time and I had a Showtime special a while back. So me and Tim Allen and the manager, we paid for a little private jet and went to the fight. It was a big thing.

"So, Showtime also invited us to dinner after the fight. We're sitting there eating dinner and I'd been drinking since about two that afternoon so I was really like, *uuuuhhh*. You know how when you were in college and you used to drink all day and you get fuzzy-headed and your breath is all beery and bad? I was just so drunk.

"I take a look behind me and at the table right behind me, there's the Mommies. The one with the dark hair. Marilyn.

"So Marilyn comes up to me and I was like, *bluuuh*. She

goes, *Why'd you say all those bad things about us, is it us you don't like?* I was like, *Oh, man, I'm just an asshole.*

"And the blonde one was just sitting there staring at me like this"—Carey crosses his arms and puckers his face into an angry pout. "She wouldn't even get up and talk to me. She was really mad.

"So I don't think I'll ever be on their show. They hate me. But that was like my most embarrassing moment. It was the worst thing. And of all the places, too: the Tyson-McNeely fight. Who would expect them to be at that? The last place you'd expect to see the Mommies is at a big, bloody heavyweight fight. I couldn't believe it."

Still, furious Mommies aside, freebies are fun and hard to turn down. It's human nature to want to be treated specially, even if it means humiliation or more work as a result. When Drew was first asked if he could make a short-notice stand-up appearance in New Orleans during Super Bowl week, he initially begged off—until he was bribed.

"It's hard, man, very hard to develop new stand-up material while you're doing a series. So when this guy says, *How'd you like to play New Orleans?* I said, *Well, I don't know, it's a lot of work. . . .* And then the guy says, *It's Super Bowl and I'll get you in the game.* So I said, *Okay, I'll do it.* And you know the only reason I did it was for the tickets," he admits.

When he first moved to Hollywood, Drew was worried to the point of paranoia that giving in to celebrity and becoming a part of the "Hollywood scene" would take away his edge, that it would make him less accessible to his core audience. But having settled into an L.A. lifestyle only seems to have given him that much more comic fodder.

Drew was now a television star and didn't turn down the perks that came with it, but he still wasn't your typical star. For one thing, you probably wouldn't find him dining out regularly at hot spots like Georgia or Drai's or Spago.

"If I want to impress my friends, I'll take them to a nice restaurant," Drew concedes. "Otherwise, it's Bob's Big Boy on Riverside Drive near the studio, or the Denny's on Sunset Boulevard, near my old apartment.

"I enjoy eating cheeseburgers and drinking beer. I'm a Budweiser man—and I only drink beer to get drunk. There's no other reason to drink. Beer doesn't taste that great. It's like coffee: Coffee tastes terrible; the only reason to drink coffee is to get that jolt.

"I used to wait tables at a fancy restaurant in Cleveland, so I know good food. But I like to read in restaurants, and if you go to Spago, they want you to eat and get out. Whereas if you go to a Bob's Big Boy and sit at the counter for five hours reading a paper, they don't care."

You won't find Drew hobnobbing with Clint Eastwood on the golf links of exclusive country clubs.

"I play the trumpet and accordion—but not at the same time. And when I'm drunk, I do modern dance."

You won't find him sitting next to Jack Nicholson courtside at Lakers basketball games.

"I'm still a fan of the Indians and Cavaliers," he says, referring to his hometown's pro baseball and hoop teams. "Oh, and the Crunch, Cleveland's soccer team—because they sent me a free soccer ball."

About the only concession he makes to the good life is an occasional taste for bubbly.

"I like Cristal champagne. For other people in L.A., that's their daily drink, but it's a special treat for me."

Nor have celebrity and a hit show made him reluctant to express his opinions through his comedy, even if the subject near and dear to his heart might make network executives squirm.

"You know, it's okay to have drive-through liquor stores, but don't even think of smoking a joint in your own house. That's against the law."

"With the way he dresses and his conservative fashion style, Drew looks like he would be a reactionary," says a friend. "But in fact, Drew's quite liberal about certain things. For example, he's very outspoken about believing marijuana should be legalized."

On the January 15 and March 5, 1997 episodes of his show, Carey briefly flashed a *Reason* T-shirt. *Reason* is a magazine of "free minds and free markets" that "examines politics, culture and ideas from a dynamic libertarian perspective."

Carey is a subscriber to *Reason* and bought the T-shirt at the magazine's Los Angeles "Evening with the Editors" in July 1996. Eighty subscribers turned out for a night of food, drink and conversation, and Drew happily posed for pictures with *Reason* senior editor Nick Gillespie.

"Wearing the *Reason* T-shirt is a deliberate *fuck you* to the people who don't get it, like, say, the corporate or network powers that be," the friend believes.

Drew also believes certain political positions are rife with self-serving hypocrisy.

"Every night people are drinking beer and whiskey," Carey says. "Every sporting event is sponsored by beer companies. How come we can have all of one but none of the other? I can't believe the government has the nerve to limit the ways I can hurt myself."

Drew points out that the war on drugs is, for the most part, a waste of money, perpetuated by politicians trying to placate their conservative constituents. "Just 'cause *those* people happen to vote. I don't think marijuana smokers get to the voting booth as often as they'd like to."

Then he questions Clinton's assertion that he didn't inhale—then or now. I mean, you know—he can't make up his mind, jogs to McDonald's . . . read the clues."

Of course, nobody's saying that just because Drew supports someone's right to smoke marijuana means he actually indulges in the drug himself. But he does have an addiction—junk food. As a kid, Drew was gangly. But according to friends, after he broke up with his would-be fiancée, he put on a lot of weight that he's yet to take off.

"The more oil and cheese the better," says Jackie Tough about her ex's culinary tastes. "Drew is the fast-food king."

And he doesn't care who knows it.

"I earned this body, man. I eat a lot of greasy foods. I love that kind of food. Denny's has my favorite food. Morning, noon and night I'm at a Denny's. My favorite meal is a hot dog with cheese and bacon.

"And for an extra dollar, they put chili on top of the whole thing. It's the meal for people who don't give a fuck anymore.

But Carey realizes the Denny's diet is not the secret to longevity. So his New Year's goal for 1997 was to get back to a more healthy fighting weight.

"I don't make resolutions—I set goals, and one of them will be to lose weight," he says. "I want to lose forty pounds."

According to the *Star* magazine, Carey went on a diet that included two potatoes a day.

"In a few more weeks I'll be looking so good you'll all be calling me the Spud Stud," Carey quipped.

Drew also attended a group called HOW, which stands for Honesty, Openness and Willingness.

"It's kind of like Overeaters Anonymous," says another member. "You attend meetings and talk about your eating habits and why you think you overeat and stuff like that."

If Drew gets too svelte, though, he'll have to update some of his better bits.

"If I put on a pair of bikini underwear, I look like a Bartlett pear with a rubber band wrapped around the bottom. It's okay, though, because I don't wear bikini underwear. Know why? Because *I* am considerate of my fellow human beings."

Overall, Drew enjoys the heightened recognizability the series has brought him, although it sometimes makes him self-conscious.

"One day I was out buying a *Playboy* and I thought, *What if somebody sees me?* Then I thought, *Who cares if they see me?* I'm single and I'm buying *Playboy*. So shut up and quit looking at me."

Other times, Drew brings on the attention himself.

"I can go crazy while driving," he admits. "I hate people who drive too slow. I'm the guy who cut you off. That was me tailgating you, honking the horn, telling you to move it along. Then I'll notice that sometimes people look at me like, *Wasn't that Drew Carey screaming at us like a maniac?*"

Although for the most part Carey is a fairly easygoing

kind of guy, his driving rage isn't completely out of character, either. Drew himself admits that his character is a lot nicer on the show than he is in real life. He can be sarcastic and profane and he doesn't have much patience with people he thinks aren't doing things the way they should be done   i.e., *his* way. Especially at work.

One woman who worked as a crew member the first season has told several people that Carey is "a bad, bad man." She refuses to elaborate other than to say, "He made my life hell."

And unlike Tim Allen, who made it a show tradition to go out with crew members after tapings, or the *Seinfeld* cast, who frequently go to Jerry's Deli in Studio City after filming is over, Drew doesn't really hang out much with his costars.

"For one thing, someone like Ryan Stiles has a whole different kind of lifestyle—he's married with kids. So he would never in a million years hang out socially with Drew, who is now a swinging bachelor," says a show source.

Indeed, Drew is not shy about showing appreciation for the ladies.

"I've seen him making out with a waitress at the Improv in the back of the main room," says a comedy club regular. "He likes the girls and comic groupies who come around. He doesn't go after women in an aggressive way, but if he finds a fan or someone who likes him, he'll go for it, no hesitation. He really is still very much a party boy."

At the 1996 Cable Ace Awards, Drew posed for photographers with that night's new best friend of the evening, Tammy Michele Cobb, whom he'd met backstage.

"I'm going to get drunk with Tammy," he happily told the paparazzi. "We might even drive to Las Vegas tonight and get married."

Even if marriage wasn't in the cards that night, one of the advantages of starring in a series is that it increases the chances of getting a date.

"Oh, yeah, it's a lot easier to get a date. But after that nothing else changes," he says with a sigh. "You're still on your own."

If Drew hasn't found Ms. Right, it's not for lack of trying. He's been spotted out on the town with several different ladies. His requirements for a companion are simple: "She has to be smart and laugh at my jokes."

When the tabloids reported that Drew was hot and heavy with cosmetology student Elena Mazzucchelli and planning to get married, Drew wasted no time in making light of the suggestion.

"It's laughably untrue," he scoffed. "We have dated, but we see other people, too."

Friends say Drew is quite happy being a bachelor. Sometimes it seems like he's reliving his Kent State days. But Drew's college-boy behavior isn't the best way to go unnoticed, and not long ago it got him into an embarrassing situation that became national news.

During the 1997 Mardi Gras in New Orleans, a fellow reveler with a handheld video captured Drew on a French Quarter balcony next to a couple of young ladies. It is apparently a Crescent City tradition that if a woman bares her breasts she'll be inundated with beads. (The hilarity of this is probably lost on you if you're sober.)

So, there's Drew on the balcony and as the video zooms in, he pulls out a $100 bill and waves it in front of one of the girls—a little incentive to flash the alcohol-addled crowd below. After a little more urging, she lifts her shirt.

Where there's a video, *Hard Copy* will not be far behind. The tabloid newsmagazine aired the footage, much to Carey's remorse. Not only did it catch Drew up close and personal, but the young woman's face was plainly visible for the world—and her family and friends—to see. Drew felt so bad, he arranged to go on *The Tonight Show* to do a public mea culpa. The apology sounded sincere.

"As much as Drew can be a sarcastic shit, he's also compassionate," says a friend. "That girl was an innocent bystander, and he felt it was his fault she got all the public notoriety. The only reason the tourist shot the video is because it was Drew Carey, so he felt responsible."

But the incident didn't curb his penchant for drinking perhaps a tad too much in public places. In April 1997,

Carey took an Orlando vacation with girlfriend Ellen Mazzucchelli, Kathy Kinney and Diedrich Bader to Walt Disney World. During their stay, Drew took golf lessons at the Disney Institute, and he and his friends visited the park by day and partied at Pleasure Island clubs at night. But one evening while visiting Epcot, Drew partied a little too heartily.

Tourist Kevin Duford was vacationing with his girlfriend when he encountered Drew and company.

"We spotted Drew sitting on the steps of the Aztec Pavilion," Duford told the *Globe*. "Drew seemed ripped; he looked like he couldn't even focus. He couldn't even stand up on his own."

Epcot officials hurried to Drew's aid, sending an employee with a wheelchair to help him leave.

"He seemed very drunk and the front of his shirt was stained. We couldn't help but laugh at this big star wearing mouse ears getting loaded into a wheelchair."

Duford immortalized Carey's embarrassing moment on film. When Diedrich Bader noticed he was taking pictures, he ran over to the Michigan tourist and his girlfriend, Betsy, and asked for the film.

"He was very nice, but worried," recalls Duford. "He promised he'd give me his autograph, and Drew's, too, if I handed over the film."

Duford was no fool. Besides the fact that the roll of film contained all the vacation photos he and his girlfriend had taken, he also knew the value of a shot of an inebriated Carey, in a mouse-ears hat ensemble, being wheeled out of the park in a chair. The tabloids live for such photos.

Another *Globe* source reported that what Duford saw represented the end of a long day of drinking.

"Drew'd been drinking throughout the World Showcase, including the German Pavilion. By the time he got to China, you could say he hit the wall."

Another incident which only recently made the papers was an excursion Drew made to a local body piercing shop called The Gauntlet, located on Melrose Avenue, a neighborhood that appeals to Gen-Xers and unsuspecting tourists.

After a night of partying, Drew went with a woman he had just met to The Gauntlet and agreed to get pierced. The employees were so thrilled to have Drew as a customer, they told just about everyone who came into the store about his visit. Eventually, reporters picked up on the story and before long it appeared in print that Drew had a newly pierced nipple. While he doesn't deny the story, he does have one gripe about its accuracy.

"They said I had my nipple pierced. Actually, I had them both pierced."

Too many more of these publicized excursions into inappropriate or risqué behavior may find Drew called on the carpet by network executives, who have invested a lot of money in him.

Thanks to the *Globe* and *Hard Copy,* Drew's frat boy rowdiness has been well documented. But less well known is his generous side.

"He doesn't make a big deal about that stuff," a friend reveals. "He feels that if you do stuff like that, you should do it because it's the right thing to do, not for publicity. A good example is a benefit Drew helped organize for an employee of the Improv.

"Antonio is a kitchen worker who's been there for twenty years. His son was shot and spent a long time in the hospital. Drew is very close to him because Antonio used to give Drew free food during his early, lean years.

"Around the beginning of 1997, Antonio's son was shot, and at first the family didn't know if the boy would survive; it was touch-and-go. Once it became apparent the boy was going to pull through, Drew helped organize a big benefit for Antonio and his son, to help with the expenses the family was facing. Hardly anybody knew that Drew had done that, because it isn't something he'd ever advertise. But that's the kind of guy Drew is.

"His stage persona is that of a sarcastic kind of guy. On the show, his interaction with Mimi makes him seem like a petty twelve-year-old. He comes across flippant and loves to do stuff to piss people off. But the truth is, he's incredibly generous and if you're in trouble and have Drew as a friend, he'll give you the shirt off his back to help you. The benefit he helped get together for Antonio is the side of Drew that only his friends get to see, but it's a big part of who he is."

Just don't tell anybody—it might ruin his image.

THIRTEEN

The future is so bright, Drew's got to wear shades. His series continues to get better: The writing is snappier and the cast members are growing into their respective roles, especially Christa Miller.

Following in the literary footsteps of Tim Allen, Jerry Seinfeld, Ellen DeGeneres and others, Drew Carey agreed to a $3 million book deal with Hyperion. Tentatively titled *Dirty Jokes and Beer,* the book is described by its publisher as Drew's "humorous philosophy of life."

Now that he's conquered television and publishing, Drew is being courted by movie studios.

"I've talked about movies, but so far it's only been talk. Right now, I'm too busy to think about doing films. But maybe one day." Actually, Drew has already appeared in a film, although it's not something he talks about much. But if you rent *Coneheads,* with Jane Curtin and Dan Aykroyd, keep your eye peeled for a familiar-looking taxi passenger.

This kind of avalanche of attention and prosperity is hard to keep in perspective for many people, but Drew has dealt with it by making fun of it.

"No, I haven't changed one bit. I'm still a common guy,

a man of the people. I get my *own* limo door; the guy doesn't have to get out and come open it for me. Sometimes, I make my own bed in hotel rooms, to give the maid a little time off. And I have my dresser put my pants on one leg at a time, just like everyone else."

Success has had one interesting effect on Drew—he's finally comfortable enough to start expanding his wardrobe beyond Kmart-brand white shirts.

"Back in the days of *The Good Life,* I played a guy who was always in the office, so naturally I was going to wear a suit and tie. And I had been wearing the same thing in my stand-up act for years. I wanted to project that. And plus, I really didn't know any better. I thought that if I ever changed clothes, nobody would recognize me or that it would be a big freaky thing for me to do.

"But I tell you, having money and success keeps you from hiding from yourself. You just have to let go of the past and be who you want to be."

Who Drew doesn't want to be is someone who's seen as a greedy opportunist. It's become a grand tradition for TV stars to chuck their original contracts and demand new deals if their show takes off and becomes a hit. The most recent example was the *Friends* strike, where the principals wanted raises to $100,000 an episode and threatened not to show up for work unless they got it. Eventually, they settled for $75,000 per episode, but not before their salary dispute was played out in the national press and generated some ill feelings from viewers who don't make $75,000 a year, much less for one week's effort. While Middle America may look upon it as greed run amok, Hollywood producers tend to be more understanding—even if in principle they disagree with the tactic.

"I think the fact that *Friends* went out and had mixed success with their movies made them realize, *I better make hay while the sun shines,*" Helford suggests. "You can't blame someone for trying to get as much as they can. But you can't blame producers for trying to hold talent to their contracts, either."

The success of a strike, of course, depends largely on the

ratings of the show and the importance of the star doing the
demanding. Kelsey Grammer staged a three-day sick-out
but was made to feel well enough to work when producers
gave him a hefty raise. But when Suzanne Somers tried to
arm-twist the *Three's Company* executives, she ended up
spending the season banished to doing phone segments at
the end of each episode.

Within weeks of the *Friends* dispute, the stars of *New
York Undercover* also refused to come into work unless they
got $75,000 per episode, better food, a personal gym and the
opportunity to direct. Producer Dick Wolfe's response was
to start auditioning for replacements. The two actors went
back to work the next day, but not without a parting shot.

"We heard Angela Lansbury made four hundred thousand
dollars an episode and Johnny Depp got fifty thousand ten
years ago on *21 Jump Street* in his third season," one of the
actors said in defense of the failed coup. "You can pay me
all the money in the world, but you can't disrespect me. It
had nothing to do with money. It's all about respect."

Actually, it's all about ratings, a fact that Drew the
businessman is well aware of.

"I get a regular five percent bump a year, and I'm happy
with that. But when I'm number one—*ba-boom*!"

Of course, as a lot of celebrities are realizing, producers
automatically share in the wealth of a successful series—
which is one reason Drew was listed as producer and
cocreator from the get-go, similar to Seinfeld's status on his
show. The drawback is possible dissension among the other
cast members, who don't automatically receive a piece of
the pie.

When NBC went to renew *Seinfeld* for the 1997–98
season, it was met with the unified front of Michael
Richards, Jason Alexander and Julia Louis-Dreyfus demanding $1 million per episode. (They ultimately agreed to
$600,000 an episode.) Part of the reason for the astronomi-
cal salary demand was the astronomical syndication package *Seinfeld* had wrought, of which Jerry got a sizable
portion, being producer and cocreator. It remains to be seen

how networks and stars like Drew Carey will try to preempt such animosity in the future.

For now, though, all is well on the set of *The Drew Carey Show*. They have found a balance and formula that works and other than minor adjustments, don't plan to fix anything that ain't broke.

"A show's always going to evolve, but the basic components are pretty much set," Carey says. "We're just going to build from what we have now and let the show take on a life of its own."

When *TV Guide* asked Carey what he promises viewers will never see on his show, Drew doesn't hesitate.

"One, you'll never see Starbucks or any kind of trendy coffeehouse on the show. Two, you'll never see trendy clothes. And three, you'll *never* see my naked butt."

Drew has come a long way from the scrawny, 123-pound teenager who enrolled at Kent State. He's come even further from the suicidal young adult who was so miserable that a bottle of pills seemed like a good solution. Although he won't get too introspective about it, Drew will allow that his unlikely journey has been pretty amazing.

"To get from where I was to where I am today is nothing short of a miracle. I'm happier than hell. If it wasn't for this, I don't know what I'd be doing. I think it is the only thing I've been good at, you know, my whole life.

"I'm one of the few people who would not quit my job if I won the lottery. But then again, I feel like I already have."

Not that Drew's life is without trauma or concerns. In 1996, Drew's stepfather, George Collingwood, died of a heart attack, and then his mother lost half a lung to cancer. But rather than fall apart, Drew has learned to take things in stride and not let bad circumstances drag him too far down—or for that matter, to let good things carry him too far up.

"Don't worry about it," he advises. "Don't let things get you down. Just forget it. Think positive. Me, I just want to have fun, no matter what. Life never gets me down anymore."

For Drew, the key is to get your enjoyment whenever and

however you can, while you can. "When it rains really hard,
I like to run stop signs just to make the cops get out of the
car. Why make the money if you can't enjoy spending it?
Make 'em stand there in the rain in a big puddle.

"*All right, you. . . . You know why I stopped you?*"
"*Yeah. . . . You know why I ran the sign?*"

Miscellany

Drew Carey/*The Drew Carey Show* Web/Usenet Sites:

  "Moon over Parma" at http://www.geocities.com/Holly-
    wood/6663/parma.htm

  "D.R.E.W." at http://newport.thirdwave.net/~kirkwww/
    drew/

  alt.tv.drew-carey

  alt.fan.drew-carey

Robert "Mad Dog" McGuire's e-mail: MarnM@AOL.com

Kathy Kinney's nickname as a child: Demon Seed

Kathy Kinney's grandmother and grandfather were cousins.

Kathy Kinney doesn't wear any makeup when not working.

Christa Miller's favorite food: take-out Chinese in New York

Ryan Stiles's most notable commercial: as a lone fan doing
the wave by himself for Nike, shot during the 1994–95
baseball strike

About the *Ghoulardi* T-shirts Drew wears on the show: *Ghoulardi* was a late-night Cleveland TV show in the 1960s. Ghoulardi was really Ernie Anderson, who is best known as the announcer for *The Carol Burnett Show* and *America's Funniest Home Videos*. He's now retired.

Drew's middle name: Allison

Drew's favorite fruits: bananas and apples

Drew's favorite snack food: Doritos with French onion dip

Drew's favorite cast member of *Friends*: "The monkey. Bring him back."